COATESVILLE AND THE
LYNCHING
OF ZACHARIAH WALKER

COATESVILLE AND THE LYNCHING
OF ZACHARIAH WALKER

DEATH IN A PENNSYLVANIA STEEL TOWN

**DENNIS B. DOWNEY
& RAYMOND M. HYSER**

THE
History
PRESS

Published by The History Press
Charleston, SC 29403
www.historypress.net

First published 2011

ISBN 978-1-5402-3027-0

Library of Congress Cataloging-in-Publication Data
Downey, Dennis B., 1952-
Coatesville and the lynching of Zachariah Walker : death in a Pennsylvania steel town /
Dennis B. Downey and Raymond M. Hyser.
p. cm.
"The present work is a substantial revision of our earlier work entitled No Crooked Death,
published by the University of Illinois Press in 1991"--Intro.
Includes bibliographical references.
ISBN 978-1-5402-3027-0
1. Lynching--Pennsylvania--Coatesville--Case studies. 2. Walker, Zachariah, d. 1911. 3.
Trials (Murder)--Pennsylvania--Coatesville. 4. Coatesville (Pa.)--Race relations. I. Hyser,
Raymond M., 1955- II. Title.
HV6462.P4D67 2011
364.1'34--dc22
2011012905

To our families

CONTENTS

ACKNOWLEDGEMENTS

Working on this project over a span of more than two decades has been a collaborative endeavor in every sense of the word. Many people have helped us along the way. Grateful appreciation is here recorded.

Barbara Erdman and Maggie Eichler offered essential help throughout this project, as did Pamela Powell and the Chester County Historical Society. Coatesville residents Eugene DiOrio and Ted Reed played a critical role in securing permission to reproduce images. Charles Hardy III of West Chester University offered wise counsel and astute judgment throughout the preparation of this manuscript. Hannah Cassilly and the editorial staff of The History Press have been patient and professional at every turn.

I also recall several wonderful conversations with Lee Carter, a retired steelworker with an abiding respect for local history. Millersville University provided generous financial support, as well as a stable environment in which to think about and do history. I also remember with great gratitude the intellectual friendship offered by the late William D. Miller and the late Monsignor William A. Kerr, both of whom valued the clarification of thought in its many forms. Finally, I express again my love and devotion to Traci and our children, Bernie, Maggie, Kara, Thomas and Anna.

—DBD

Acknowledgements

I wish to thank my colleagues at James Madison University for their support and guidance over the years. My children, Kelsey, Marshall and Christopher, made me see the world differently through their boundless joy and love. The greatest debt is owed to Pamela, whose generous portions of love, patience and good humor were more than anyone could ask.

—RMH

INTRODUCTION

During the first week in August 1911, an itinerant African American minister preached a religious revival at the Tabernacle Baptist Church in Coatesville, Pennsylvania. His name was Prophet Andrew Jones, "the colored prophet," according to the local newspaper, and nothing is known of him except this: he claimed that God had ordained him with the gift to foretell the future. Jones informed the all-black congregation that he had correctly predicted such diverse tragedies as the Johnstown flood, the Baltimore fire and the San Francisco earthquake. Now, in the closing moments of his weeklong crusade, the evangelist said he had a special message for the black citizens of Coatesville. A "great misfortune was about to fall on the town," he predicted, and in this time of trial and tribulation they would do well to remember that the meek *shall* inherit the earth. The *Coatesville Record* reported that Jones counseled local blacks to "make no attempt at violence although they would be sorely tested."

Little more than a week later, on a warm Sunday evening, a black man named Zachariah Walker was murdered on the edge of town, burned alive as a crowd of several thousand people looked on fascinated by the spectacle. Three times he attempted to free himself, only to be pushed back onto his funeral pyre by young men closest to the flames. No one stood against the mob, and some spectators waited hours for the ashes to cool so they could retrieve souvenir bone fragments. Walker's last words were a mournful plea to his captors: "Don't give me no crooked death because I'm not white."

The next morning, young boys sold pieces of Walker's body on downtown street corners.

Not surprisingly, the death of Zachariah Walker focused national and international attention on this Pennsylvania steel town and its nearly twelve thousand inhabitants. Commentators familiar with the commonplace nature of racial lynching in turn-of-the-century America remarked on the brutal manner of death and on the oddity of this incident's geographic location in a northern industrial town rather than the American South. Former president Theodore Roosevelt was among the host of critics who rebuked townsfolk for their failure to prevent the lynching. In the midst of blistering criticism, Coatesville's residents joined ranks in what a county judge criticized as a "conspiracy of silence" that thwarted the efforts of prosecutors to bring the perpetrators to justice. On the first anniversary of the lynching, social reformer John Jay Chapman traveled to Coatesville to conduct a memorial service, commemorating what he called "an American tragedy." No more than a half dozen people attended the gathering.

Published on the occasion of the 100th anniversary of Zachariah Walker's death, this narrative seeks to tell the story of what happened and why it is of enduring significance. In some respects, the present work is a substantial revision of our earlier work entitled *No Crooked Death*, published by the University of Illinois Press in 1991. That earlier book, no longer in print, represented a more detailed and scholarly approach to the subject, seeking to place the Coatesville lynching in the context of the developing scholarly discourse on lynching and racial violence in American history. As a scholarly case study, *No Crooked Death* has held up well and received its own notoriety over the past two decades.

In this revised and substantially altered text, however, we have attempted to update and make more accessible to a general audience the compelling and controversial saga of Zach Walker's brief life and tragic death in a Pennsylvania steel town. We have retained the basic narrative found in *No Crooked Death*, but we have omitted intentionally some of the detail and recast portions of the larger contextual analysis while retaining the sense of historical drama found in this individual historical event. Local controversy surrounding the 2006 dedication of a historical marker, which we discuss in the Afterword, provides fresh evidence of how the death of Zachariah Walker has been interwoven in the fabric of community relations in Coatesville and the surrounding area.

"Ask big questions of small places," historian Charles Joyner once advised. As in the earlier work, that is our intention in this version of the story. In many respects, the lynching of Zachariah Walker is freighted with meaning—for the residents of Coatesville and for others interested in the American past. Walker's death at the hands of a mob typifies what historians now call a "spectacle lynching." Mobs of thousands watched grotesque rituals of violence that were often accompanied by unusual and stylized acts of mutilation and human desecration. Not only did some bystanders wait hours to retrieve relics, but others took photographs to remember the event long after it had passed. Perhaps Michael Pfeifer put it best when he observed that lynching was a form of "rough justice" that reveals important features of individual and community sentiments on matters of race and rights. Lynching was a crime, a form of extralegal violence that rarely was punished. While its proponents could defend the practice as understandable and even necessary, its critics more often condemned the practice of mob violence with impunity as a betrayal of democracy and any sense of decency. Too often in the history of lynching, due process under law received little respect as the mob stirred to action. Not too many years before the Coatesville incident, Mark Twain struck at the heart of the matter in an essay entitled "The United States of Lyncherdom," when he castigated those who lacked the moral courage to stand against the mob.

This narrative tells the story of one death by lynching in one Pennsylvania steel town at the dawn of the twentieth century. It also offers an assessment of the social world in which this episode of mob violence occurred. Contrary to expectations, Coatesville was not a small town in the rural South, the accustomed locale for such events. Rather, Coatesville was a prosperous northern steel town riding the crest of the Industrial Revolution and material progress. As in other industrial towns across America, over the previous decade Coatesville had experienced a massive influx of newcomers, southern and eastern European immigrants and black migrants from the American South. Zachariah Walker was one such newcomer from rural Virginia, and he had few formal ties to the larger community, a place divided along class, ethnic and racial lines. All of these factors are relevant in the drama that played out "that quiet Sabbath evening," to borrow W.E.B. Du Bois's phrase, one hundred years ago.

In a very particular sense, the Walker lynching and its aftermath redefined community in Coatesville. Without wishing to sensationalize what remains

Introduction

a sensitive subject, our hope is that readers will find in this narrative both a compelling story and rich insights into the complexity of human experience in early twentieth-century America. At the heart of this story is a social drama in one place at one time. But this is a story that continues to reverberate and lend meaning to our understanding of the human condition. History is, after all, something that happens to people, and the human condition is the heart of historical significance.

Chapter 1
"That Quiet Sabbath Evening"

Zachariah Walker was lured from his home in rural Stanardsville, Virginia, by the availability of jobs for unskilled workers and the general industrial prosperity of the North. Numerous labor agents, working to recruit blacks for the steel mills, also portrayed the area as idyllic, a heaven on earth. Another enticing feature was the absence of Jim Crow segregation laws, which led Walker, and so many other blacks, to believe that there was a greater sense of freedom in the North. By 1911, he had found work as a laborer, an obscure lever-puller, in the Worth Brothers Steel Company, located in Coatesville, Pennsylvania. Walker would soon learn, however, that his new home was hardly the Promised Land he sought.

Coatesville is situated along the west branch of the Brandywine Creek in Chester County, approximately forty miles west of Philadelphia and twenty miles north of the Maryland border, surrounded by some of the best farmland in the country. It was established as a post office in 1812 and took its name from the Irish Quaker postmaster, Moses Coates, who owned a large tract of land from which the town developed. In 1818, an iron foundry was built along the creek, and throughout the nineteenth century, Coatesville developed into a small industrial community.

Although the iron mills flourished in the valley, they were closely tied to the ebb and flow of the new economic order and eventually converted to steel production, a rapidly expanding industry. Coatesville never approximated the size of Pittsburgh or Bethlehem, remaining a middling steel town to this day.

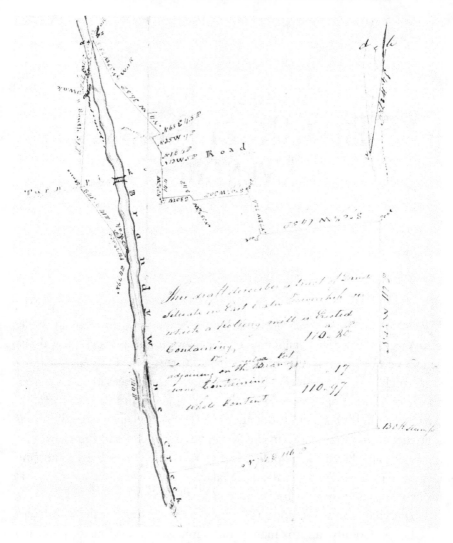

A copy of the first known land draft, Lukens Steel in Coatesville, 1810. *Courtesy of the Lukens Archives and the Chester County Historical Society.*

Two sprawling steel mills dominated the local economy and social relations in 1911. The Worth Brothers Steel Company was the largest, employing nearly 1,500 workers. The Lukens Steel and Iron Company, significantly smaller, was nonetheless the second leading employer in the borough. Both companies had their operations along the banks of Brandywine Creek, with Lukens headquartered within the borough and Worth Brothers situated in

A view of the Lukens Rolling Mill, Coatesville, circa 1882. *Courtesy of the Lukens Archives and the Chester County Historical Society.*

Workers assembled at a Lukens mill site, Coatesville, circa 1870. *Courtesy of the Lukens Archives and the Chester County Historical Society.*

Old mill at Lukens Steel, circa 1887. *Courtesy of the Chester County Historical Society.*

East Fallowfield Township, just beyond the southern limits of Coatesville. Brandywine Creek formed a north–south axis that bisected the borough; Main Street, sometimes called the Lincoln Highway, formed an east–west axis. The steel mills, long the focal point of community life, literally towered over the landscape. Steel was the lifeblood of Coatesville, and it could be seen, heard and smelled in every corner of the town. Local residents felt reassured when black, sooty smoke hung in the valley, for it meant the mills were running and times were prosperous.

By the summer of 1911, Coatesville had some pressing problems. Although a few of the borough's streets were paved or macadamized, most were dirt with a "trap rock" dressing spread over the top. A stretch of several hundred yards along Main Street was known as the "flats" and became flooded after each rainstorm, and during the winter, the streets became impassable rutted quagmires. In the summer, even on the hottest days and despite the efforts of the Washington and Brandywine fire companies, which sprinkled water on the streets, residents were compelled to keep their doors and windows closed to prevent clouds of dust from settling inside their homes and businesses. If the streets were going to be repaired or oiled, local residents would have to pay the entire expense—which they were apparently unwilling (or unable) to do. Automobiles, so novel in Coatesville that to drive one on a town street guaranteed a newspaper headline, created havoc, as most drivers went too fast, disobeyed street courtesy and terrorized pedestrians and those on horseback. The police could do little to control the mayhem.

Another problem was the borough's woefully inadequate supply of drinking water, which was often brown with dirt, forcing residents to let foreign particles settle before they could quench their thirst. In the spring, they had to contend with live tadpoles and small fish flowing with the water from the faucets. More serious than the water shortages was the constant threat of typhoid fever epidemics due to inadequate filtration and treatment facilities. Also, garbage was left to accumulate in the alleys and side streets, attracting packs of dogs. Once a year, the police embarked on a hunt, tracking down and killing all unleashed dogs in the borough.

Despite these problems, Coatesville enjoyed the beginnings of an economic resurgence during the summer of 1911. For the first time since the Panic of 1907, which had practically crippled the town's steel productivity, the mills were operating at near capacity. There also seemed to be a strong community bond and an increase in local boosterism. Coatesville touted its electrically lighted "White Way," a stretch of Main Street in the downtown business district that was, in the opinion of local residents, "better lighted than Broadway in New York." The Harvest Home Festival, a weeklong series of activities, was scheduled for mid-August to celebrate the coming agricultural harvest as well as the revival of the steel mills. Shops, businesses and banks were closed on Thursday, August 10, as the business community hosted a special day of events. Thousands attended a parade, complete with automobiles, and there were various athletic contests (including a tug of war between the two fire companies), an automobile race and musical productions. Someone even thrilled the crowd by parachuting out of a hot air balloon as it floated over the town.

Zachariah Walker may have worked in Coatesville, but he did not live there. Rather, he coexisted with recent European immigrants and fellow southern blacks in the Spruces, a collection of shacks that passed as homes on a bluff overlooking the sprawling steel mills. The Spruces was located just beyond Brandywine Creek in East Fallowfield Township, nearly one mile from downtown Coatesville. Inhabitants of this area purchased food and supplies in Bernardtown, a cluster of small stores at the foot of the hill, except on Saturdays, when they flocked to the taverns and stores in the borough. On August 12, the final day of the Harvest Home Festival, Walker and his friend Oscar Starkey were in Coatesville. The two men milled around Main Street near the Smith Hotel, drinking gin for most of the day. This was a common Saturday occurrence among immigrants and blacks, especially after the "ghost walked" on Friday (the steelworkers' term for payday). The throngs were often so large that pedestrians and vehicles could barely pass along Main Street and First Avenue. Drunks jeered and made gestures at passersby, and fights broke out with the slightest provocation. Native white residents, angered by the decline in civility and the increase in arrests, violent crime and property damage, avoided the shopping district after noon (much to the chagrin of shopkeepers). The six-man Coatesville police force was hard-pressed to maintain some semblance of order. On Saturday nights, the town lockup, sometimes affectionately called "Fort Jumbo" in honor of the portly police chief, was usually filled with men sleeping off their daylong drinking binges. The town newspapers protested the usual Saturday behavior, particularly when inebriated workers carried concealed firearms and threatened the borough's respectable citizens, but by the summer of 1911 the ritual was firmly in place.

As twilight fell on that Saturday in August, an intoxicated Zachariah Walker parted company with Oscar Starkey, stopped by the Smith Hotel for more liquor and then staggered down First Avenue toward his shack in the Spruces. Just across the covered bridge that spanned Brandywine Creek beyond the Worth Brothers mill, he came across two Polish workers. By his own admission, Walker was "feeling pretty good," and he decided to have some fun with the two foreigners. He removed a revolver that was tucked into his pants and fired several shots in their general direction. Although the bullets sailed over their heads, they were understandably terrified and ran screaming down the road. Walker, delighted and amused that he could cause such panic with so little effort, tucked the pistol back into his pants and continued on his way, laughing and talking loudly to himself.

The commotion attracted the attention of Edgar Rice, a commissioned coal and iron policeman of the Worth Brothers Steel Company who was on duty at the company substation Walker had passed only a few minutes

Main Street in downtown Coatesville, 1911. *Courtesy of the Chester County Historical Society.*

earlier. Rice left his post at about 9:00 p.m., crossed the covered bridge and proceeded down Youngsburg Road to investigate the noise. He encountered Walker, staggering along in the darkness, and asked him a few questions before accusing him of firing the shots. Walker vehemently denied the accusation and tried to plead his case, but Rice refused to listen. Although no weapon was visible, Rice placed Walker under arrest "for carrying concealed weapons." When Rice insisted on searching for the pistol, Walker refused to cooperate. "I protested knowing that I had a gun and was afraid of the penalty," he said later. Rice then attempted to escort the drunken man back to the company guardhouse, but Walker, by his own admission, "got a little sassy with him," leaning against Rice as the police officer tried to restrain him.

Rice, noted for his gentle and patient demeanor, particularly with drunks, suddenly became more aggressive and thundered, "Quit leaning against me. If you don't come with me, I will hit you over the head with this club." To reinforce the warning, he drew his nightstick and squared off against Walker, who lost his balance and stumbled into Rice yelling, "Hit me and I will kill you!" The company policeman, his patience gone, was attempting to guide Walker down the hill when the black man panicked and, his mind clouded with alcohol, began to resist a perceived attack. The two started to "tussle," and Walker threw several wild punches. Rice then clubbed him a number

A view of Worth Brothers steel mill, 1911, where Zachariah Walker was employed. *Courtesy of the Chester County Historical Society.*

of times with his nightstick before Walker, in his own words, "tore it out of his hand." Rice reached instinctively for his police revolver and lunged toward Walker. But Walker pulled out his own pistol and fired a shot at Rice that sent him reeling down the hill. Walker then proceeded to fire two more shots, both of which tore into Rice's back and through his body. Severely wounded, Rice made it to the bottom of the hill and collapsed on the porch of Sayleon Miclebreck's small store. A few moments later, one of the most popular men in Coatesville was dead.

Although no one actually witnessed the Rice-Walker confrontation, a small group of immigrants from the area now gathered near the road and watched Walker search frantically for his hat, which he had lost during the fight. Seemingly unfazed by what he had done, Walker asked a "Hunkie" for a match so he could look for his hat. He found Rice's police revolver instead and tucked it into his pants, then grabbed a bystander's hat and fled the scene. He went first to his shanty, then walked peacefully to the crest of the bluff overlooking the Brandywine Creek and sat down to drink some more gin.

William Whitesides, a member of the Worth Brothers police force and Rice's brother-in-law, was the first to arrive at Miclebreck's store. "My God, it is Edgar," was all Whitesides could say when he saw the body lying motionless in a pool of blood. He quickly telephoned the police department, the Brandywine Fire Company and the Rice family to tell them of Edgar's tragic death. Despite the late hour—it was almost 10:00 p.m.—word of the killing raced through the borough like heat lightning across a summer night's sky. Coatesville residents flocked into the streets to discuss the incident and await further news. Several blocks of Main Street and First Avenue were crowded with excited people, with many expressing grief over the death of the popular policeman. All available automobiles, including the "big touring car" of William and Sharpless Worth, owners of the steel mill, were pressed into service to search for Rice's assailant. Teams of horses were hitched to wagons and carriages to transport men to the scene of the crime, and Police Chief Charles E. Umsted called on the two steel companies' police forces for assistance. By 11:00 p.m., less than one hour after Rice's murder was publicly announced, First Avenue all the way to Bernardtown was choked with vehicles, curious townsfolk and members of various search parties.

A hasty search for clues at the murder site produced Walker's hat. Several immigrants—who clearly stated that they had not witnessed the murder—provided a sketchy description of Walker and the general location of his shack. Oscar Starkey, the two Polish men who had been shot at by Walker and a few others were held as witnesses in the Coatesville jail. The police went to Walker's shack, but all they found was a cache of letters. Using automobiles and fast, horse-drawn carriages, they proceeded to race down country roads looking for evidence of Walker's whereabouts. However, their search was hampered by darkness, a summer storm that brought a driving rain to the valley and their own fatigue. Several times during the night the various posses returned to Coatesville for dry clothes and something warm to drink. Many of the residents sent scurrying home by the storm pledged their assistance for Sunday morning, should the villain still be at large.

From his vantage point on the bluff, Walker observed the frenzy of activity near the covered bridge: the Worth brothers' automobile, the police search parties, the crowds. He even sat there throughout the downpour, "all the time people were going up and down the road." About 1:00 a.m., according to Walker, "it became quieter," and he went briefly to his shanty before striking out for the countryside south of town. "Being very sleepy and intoxicated," he slipped into the haymow of Norm Entrekin's barn, where he slept for the remainder of the night. Early Sunday morning, a boy named Louis Townsend discovered Walker while collecting eggs. Townsend informed farm laborer Alexander Markley that a black man was in the barn, and Markley passed the information to Daniel McInerney and John Cochran, two Coatesville citizens who were searching for Walker in a nearby field. In the meantime, Walker managed to slip out of the barn and was walking down a country road when McInerney and Cochran attempted to stop him. Neither man had a weapon, nor did they call for police assistance. Walker knocked Cochran unconscious with a single blow to the head and then stuck a pistol in McInerney's chest and pulled the trigger. Fortunately for McInerney, the gun misfired, and he escaped unscathed. (The police chief later reported that the firing pin in Walker's revolver had struck the bullet, which had failed to discharge.) Walker ran into Robert Faddis's woods nearby and hid in a cherry tree where, fatigued and frightened, a sense of panic began to grip him. Having recovered from their flirtation with death, Cochran and McInerney telephoned the Brandywine Fire Company and the police station and described their altercation with Walker and the general direction of his escape.

The police and fire company reacted quickly to the news that Walker had been located in East Fallowfield Township. Umsted and three police officers, along with Chester County district attorney Robert S. Gawthrop, were driven to the Entrekin farm in the Worths' touring car. The trustees of the Brandywine Fire Company, at the behest of the police department, ordered their best team of horses hitched to the police patrol wagon to take a posse of firemen to the farm. Numerous rifles and shotguns were secured from a local gunsmith so that each man in the posse would be armed. The police made a thorough search of the woods and cornfields where Walker was last seen but could not locate him. Walker later noted how close the police had come: "I saw you, Umsted, in your uniform come down the road in the automobile and heard the crowd say they were going to surround the woods...you were not twenty feet away from me, at one time in the woods Sunday afternoon." After combing the countryside for a few hours, the police force abandoned the search at about noon and returned to Coatesville. Seven members of the Brandywine Fire Company, led by aviator Al Berry (who operated the hot air balloon concession during the Harvest Home Festival), continued the manhunt with the assistance of some heavily armed men from the township.

Later that afternoon, a pistol shot rang out from Faddis's woods, and two foreigners ran from the area claiming that "a black man shot out of a tree" at them. The posse from the fire company raced across two fields and surrounded the woods. "I saw Walker up a tree," Al Berry recalled. "I started

A fire department steamer on Main Street, Coatesville, circa 1906. Notice the earthen pavement. *Courtesy of the Chester County Historical Society.*

to cover him with my gun and ordered him to come down." Some of the men moved cautiously, and at a safe distance, to surround the tree, mindful that Walker was said to be carrying a gun. "I knew it was all up with me," Walker later confessed. "I thought I would end it all and send a bullet in the back of my head." He pointed the pistol at his temple and fired, which caused him to lose his balance and fall from the tree. Berry ran to Walker's side and rolled him over, immediately noticing a large bullet wound from behind the ear to the mouth. Walker was alive but unconscious and bleeding profusely, his jawbone shattered. Berry fired his shotgun twice to notify the others of Walker's capture. Some members of the search party later claimed that the shots were part of a gun battle involving Walker. The Pennsylvania State Police report on the incident substantially corroborated the attempted suicide but also noted that one witness believed a member of the search party had "shot Walker with a rifle, causing him to fall from the tree." As some of the men gathered around, Berry rummaged through Walker's pockets and found a flask of whiskey, which he poured down the victim's throat in an attempt to revive him. When this failed, Berry resumed his search and found Rice's "blue-barrelled, blue steel" police revolver in Walker's right coat pocket. Another pistol, apparently Walker's, was discovered at the foot of the tree.

Al Berry ordered the firemen to take the fugitive to the patrol wagon and turn him over to the police. When several of them grabbed Walker's feet and began dragging the unconscious, bleeding man toward the road, Berry screamed, "Pick him up as you ought to; remember the man is human." The men made a litter out of their rifles and laid Walker across it. As they picked him up, someone yelled out, "Let us lynch the Son of a Bitch while we have him here." Berry responded by pointing his shotgun at the men and declaring that there would be no lynching as long as he was responsible for Walker. "The man that tries to do any lynching, I will shoot," he boldly threatened. Muttered words of dissatisfaction were heard as Walker was carried to the road. Since the patrol wagon had earlier returned to Coatesville with the police, the firemen stopped Ellis Ridgeway, who was passing by, and demanded the use of his automobile to transport Walker to the police station. Ridgeway refused, arguing that Walker was black and a criminal and his blood would soil the car. Following a heated argument, he reluctantly agreed to take Walker and several firemen to Coatesville. The remainder of the search party either waited for the patrol wagon to return or walked back to town, a distance of several miles.

News of Walker's capture spread quickly throughout the borough. A sizable crowd had gathered at the Brandywine Fire Company, anxiously awaiting information on the search, and when they were informed at about 3:00 p.m. that Walker had been apprehended, they immediately began celebrating. They cheered wildly as the Ridgeway automobile with Walker stretched across the back seat passed the fire station, and several hundred of them ran behind the car while others spread the word that Rice's murderer had been captured. One newspaper reported that "thousands of persons, who had made up the posses that had searched the woods and corn fields of the vicinity since Saturday, learning of his capture, surrounded the lockup." (The numbers likely were exaggerated, although perhaps as many as two thousand people did swarm around the automobile when it arrived at the jail.) Adding to the confusion of the moment, the police station was locked and the posse had to remain in the street for several minutes until Umsted arrived. The crowd became more threatening as it pressed closer to the car, and when people learned that Walker was only unconscious, not dead, someone shouted out, "That man ought to be lynched," and another said, "That damned nigger ought to be lynched."

Walker regained consciousness as the police arrived and, according to a witness, "made motions for the officers to kill him." This delighted the crowd and prompted several people to shout that the police should grant his wish. Instead, Walker was taken into the lockup and placed on the floor of a cell. Before entering the station, Chief Umsted told the crowd that the prisoner was dead, but most people suspected that he was lying in an attempt to get them to disperse, so they remained outside the station, their numbers swelling as word of Walker's capture spread. The two Polish men who had been detained as witnesses were released after positively identifying Walker as the man who had terrified them on the Youngsburg Road; one of them was even able to identify the hat Walker had taken the previous night. Oscar Starkey was also released from custody. The revolvers found on Walker's person were given to the authorities, and Umsted immediately recognized Rice's police pistol. Those in charge were certain that Rice's assailant had been captured.

Dr. Artinis Carmichael was brought in to examine Walker's head wound and determined that it was not life threatening. He did advise, however, that the prisoner be taken to the hospital for medical treatment to remove the bullet still lodged in his jaw. The police chief agreed to transport Walker to the Coatesville Hospital and went outside to address the crowd. Again he told those gathered that Walker was dead and that the district attorney had demanded the mob disperse; again he was ignored. "Shouts of hurrahs went up from the crowd" as Walker was carried out, "and then they applauded the captors," the *Coatesville Record* reported. The entire police force and several deputized citizens, armed with shotguns, escorted the prisoner to the hospital, located a mile from the business district atop a knoll overlooking the steel mills.

At about four o'clock that afternoon, Walker came out of surgery and was placed in a private room while still heavily sedated. Since he was a prisoner and earlier had attempted suicide, precautionary measures were taken to ensure his safety. Walker's right ankle was shackled to the post of the iron hospital bed with a pair of police handcuffs, and he was placed in a canvas straitjacket, which was buckled to the four corners of the bed, "to keep him from getting his hands up to his head and tear[ing] the bandage off" or attempting suicide again. A police officer, Stanley Howe, was left to guard him.

Once Walker regained consciousness, Chief Umsted and District Attorney Gawthrop joined Officer Howe, who was already questioning the prisoner. Although he was still in shock and drowsy from the sedation, Walker gave them his account of the altercation with Edgar Rice. These three men were the only ones to hear Walker's statement, which amounted to a confession. He recounted the attempted arrest, the fight that ensued and Rice's reaching for his revolver. "I was too quick for him," Walker stated. "I had my gun out first and fired two shots." He insisted, however, that he had shot Rice in self-defense, that Rice had attacked him without cause. But he went on to boast, "I killed him easy." Walker concluded with a recollection of his flight and his attempted suicide while in the cherry tree. Umsted and Gawthrop left the hospital at about six o'clock, instructing Howe "to prevent him [Walker] from doing any further injury to himself." Apparently, Howe was not explicitly ordered to protect Walker from others, despite the vocal hostility of the crowds throughout the day.

Some of the people who had earlier pressed near the police station now gathered along Main Street, between First and Second Avenues, and more than one hundred men and boys stood outside the Brandywine Fire Company, "as if assembling for a holiday occasion." Residents from surrounding communities rode the trolleys into Coatesville to inspect the scene, their curiosity fueled by widespread rumors about the fate of Rice's murderer. By early evening, several blocks of Main Street from the fire station to the World in Motion amusement center were congested, and on a number of occasions the Brandywine Fire Company ordered people in the street to clear a path for vehicular traffic and pedestrians. One block away, on Second Avenue, a small crowd stood outside Sharp's Drugstore listening to the Salvation Army Band's Sunday evening summer concert. Inside the Coatesville Candy Company, several friends of Vincent Rice drank sodas and discussed the violent death of their friend's father. Other residents of the borough attended the usual Sunday evening religious services at various churches. Yet, no matter where or why people gathered on "that quiet Sabbath evening," the topic of conversation was "the cold-blooded murder of ex-Policeman Rice." Before long, impatience and a heightened sense of anxiety would galvanize the crowd on Main Street toward some form of action.

Having returned from the hospital and a visit to the site of Walker's capture, Umsted and Gawthrop mingled with the people on Main Street. It was about 7:00 p.m. Although Gawthrop heard threats against Walker, he concluded that "nothing was out of the ordinary," since "that kind of talk is always apt to be heard in a town after such a crime has occurred." The district attorney believed that the residents of Coatesville might talk about harming Rice's killer but would not follow their words with action. And with darkness approaching, he expected that people would soon return to their homes. He did take one precaution, however, asking that each hotel bar not serve alcohol until Tuesday to limit the possibility of violence. Then, concluding that "everything was quiet and orderly" in Coatesville, he caught the eight o'clock trolley (the last one that night) to his home in West Chester.

A 1906 view of Main Street and the Conestoga Trolley Line that ran between West Chester and Coatesville. *Courtesy of the Frank Pennegar Collection and the Chester County Historical Society.*

What Gawthrop had not observed was the feeling of outrage among those who had visited the Rice home throughout the afternoon and evening to express their condolences to the family. Seeing the grieving widow and her four children provoked their ire, but it was the public display of Rice's body that most affected the visitors. "Everyone talked about seeing him and how nice he looked, and about the smile that was on his face," Al Berry recalled. Many of them stood outside the West End home in a state of disbelief, talking about the tragedy and what would become of the man's family.

Edgar Rice had endeared himself to many of Coatesville's residents by his gentle demeanor and humane concern for the welfare of others, especially the steelworkers and their families. For several years, he was a member of the borough police force, though he was not a typical borough police officer. He made effective use of his portly stature and popularity to limit illegal activity on his beat, making few arrests and rarely resorting to violence when apprehending a criminal. Rice was said to have frequently assisted drunken unfortunates, guiding them home "instead of taking them to the lockup, thus saving wives and children the imposition of a fine and disgrace." He was also a well-known member of the Brandywine Fire Company, the social and political hub of Coatesville. Although Rice lost a 1908 election (by 48 votes out of 1,432 cast) for town constable to longtime incumbent Charles E. Umsted, he had demonstrated surprising political strength as a Democratic candidate in the staunchly Republican town. Two years later, after he was suddenly discharged from the police force for taking "an active part in politics" against the reigning political faction, he joined the Worth Brothers as a company policeman and served faithfully until that fateful Saturday evening confrontation with Zachariah Walker.

As District Attorney Gawthrop left for West Chester, having also failed to notice the crowd's increasing agitation as a result of the police chief's behavior, Umsted was standing in front of the Brandywine Fire Company with a reporter from the *Coatesville Record*. Politically adroit and nimble enough to survive the seething cauldron of Coatesville politics, "Jummy," as he was called, took one look at the crowd and sensed an opportunity to increase his popularity. He began to talk about Walker's capture and confession in such a loud voice that virtually everyone nearby could hear him. As people pressed closer to catch his every word, an officer of the fire company came out to ask the police chief to stop blocking the pavement—to which Umsted flippantly replied, "I must be drawing flies!" One of the things that Umsted failed to mention was Walker's claim that he had killed Rice in self-defense; in fact, he suggested that Walker had *boasted* about killing Rice—a comment that was sure to provoke the several hundred bystanders. Umsted concluded with the remark, "It would be the devil if somebody should happen to go after that fellow…Gentlemen, allow me to say that I am not going to get hurt." As he circulated throughout Coatesville that evening, he told of Walker's confession to anyone willing to listen. Several people in the crowd near the fire company soon began talking about "this nigger and what ought to be done with him." Clearly, Umsted's behavior had done nothing to calm fears or subdue the more aggressive members of the crowd.

Throughout the evening, groups of people would venture to the hospital to satisfy their curiosity about Walker's condition and attempt to see the prisoner. Officer Howe managed to turn most of them away before they entered the building, but not before he informed them that Walker would probably live. At about 7:00 p.m., while Umsted was regaling the crowd along Main Street with Walker's confession and Gawthrop was preparing to head home, one of the two black policemen in the borough, John Jackson, visited with Howe for an hour in Walker's room. Hospital orderly John Temple, himself a black man, was present while the officers discussed the possibility of a lynching and how easily Walker could be taken from his room on the first floor. When Jackson asked Howe what he would do if a mob stormed the hospital intent on lynching Walker, Howe supposedly replied, "I would get back in the closet and let them get the son of a bitch." Temple agreed: "I will get in some closet too. I will not take a chance." When Jackson left the hospital a short time later, he was aware that a crowd had gathered on the hospital lawn and prudently decided that he did not want to be nearby if something happened.

Four other people managed to enter the hospital and observe Walker in his private room. Vincent Rice, the son of the deceased police officer, and a friend named Norman Price convinced Howe to let them in, and they apparently discussed the murder with Walker. During this decidedly unusual conversation, Howe, who had been ordered to protect the prisoner, interjected, "A man that will do a thing like that ought to be hung." At about eight o'clock, Al Berry and William Gilbert arrived at the hospital to ascertain the location of the prisoner's room; they were allowed inside, presumably because Berry had aided in Walker's capture. The men chatted for a few minutes about the mistake Walker had made in shooting Edgar

Rice, and then Berry, who commented that he had prevented a lynching earlier in the day, reportedly said, "The mistake made was that they ought to have shot the son of a bitch out at the tree" when they had the chance. While Gilbert and Berry were still in the room, Dr. Carmichael telephoned instructions that Walker was to have no visitors. After informing the two that the prisoner would live, Officer Howe asked them to leave.

As Gilbert and Berry walked along the "flats" on West Main Street near the gashouse, they encountered a gang of about fifty boys and young men who were headed for the hospital. When the two asked what the group's intentions were, several members boldly stated that they were going to lynch Walker. Having just returned from the hospital, Gilbert offered some advice. "It would be a cinch to get the nigger," he suggested, because "there was only one man on duty and that was Officer Howe." Berry interrupted, insisting that a larger body of men was needed. He stated that "there ought to be more men than this. There ought to be 500 go." So with Gilbert and Berry in the lead, the group returned to the fire station to gather additional supporters.

It was now nearly nine o'clock, and the crowds along Main Street were growing weary of all the talk. When a horse-drawn ambulance was seen heading toward the hospital, word quickly circulated that Walker was about to be whisked away to West Chester. (Some people also may have overheard Richard Gibney, chairman of the borough council's police committee, advise Umsted to do just that, to which Umsted replied that the talk of lynching Walker was "all hot air.") But it was a teenager's brief speech in front of the Brandywine Fire Company—during which he repeated William Gilbert's comments—that finally incited the mob to action. Within a matter of minutes, as one witness recalled, "the people were running in every direction; people was coming from every direction." As evening church services were dismissed—or brought to a hasty conclusion by the abrupt departure of members of the congregation—people flocked to join the mob. Men, women and children swelled the ranks until there were, by some estimates, as many as two thousand people pressed shoulder to shoulder along the narrow street leading to the hospital. The constable of neighboring West Brandywine Township received a telephone call from someone who said, "You had better come down and see the fun."

At the hospital gates, angry members of the mob stopped a departing horse-drawn ambulance and, thinking that Walker was inside, frantically searched it, frightening the driver and Dr. H.A. Graves, as well as the horses. The vehicle was empty, having already discharged its sole passenger (an injured railroad worker). Much of the crowd then proceeded up the steeply graded hospital lane and scattered over the knoll. At this point, they appeared to be leaderless, but verbally, and by their physical presence, they supported some bold actions.

Alerted by an off-duty nurse that "there was a big crowd coming toward the hospital," Officer Howe instructed Miss Lena Townsend, superintendent of the hospital and a new resident of Coatesville, to telephone police headquarters and ask for help. During the next few minutes, she tried several times but got no answer; she also called two hotels in town trying to locate Chief Umsted or any police officer, to no avail. After observing that Walker was unaware of the pending danger, Howe began a halfhearted, panicky effort to secure the building: he locked windows, drew curtains and even closed the door to Walker's room, but he neglected to lock the doors of the building. He then took the telephone from Miss Townsend and called the three major hotels—the Stephenson, Speakman and Coatesville—the two fire companies and the telephone operator, leaving frantic messages for the absent police chief. Meanwhile, Miss Townsend alertly locked the glass double doors of the hospital, just as a few people moved onto the front porch.

The Stephenson House, a popular gathering place on Main Street, Coatesville. *Courtesy of the Chester County Historical Society.*

Following his public discourse on Walker's confession, Charles Umsted had walked the short distance from the Brandywine Fire Company to the office of Squire Myer, the justice of the peace. Umsted, along with the rest of the Coatesville police force, seemed unconcerned that any harm might come to Edgar Rice's killer. At about eight o'clock, the police chief and several other men, including Norman Wood, a reporter for the *Record*, went into Myer's office to sit down and rest. Umsted had not slept in thirty-six hours and had not changed his clothes since Saturday evening's rainstorm. He seemed visibly fatigued but was nonchalant about the restive crowds and would later claim that he "did not have an inkling" of the mob's desires. However, testimony revealed that, as events escalated on the streets, several prominent townspeople visited Umsted in Myer's office and told him of the increasingly tense situation in Coatesville. Albert Jackson, chief of police for the Lukens Iron and Steel Company, learned that "only Stanley Howe" was in the hospital and offered "any assistance" to protect Walker from the angry crowd. Umsted refused the help, cryptically replying, "If they get him they will have to get him." Mordecai Markward, the assistant chief of the Brandywine Fire Company and one of the men who had helped capture Walker, burst in and bluntly told Umsted, "It looks bad out there now. Things look desperate. Look at that crowd going over the flats right now: They are going to lynch that man now." The chief appeared indifferent and waved his hands at Markward in disgust. "That is all hot air," he said, reiterating a statement made earlier in the day that "there is no danger."

Umsted remained in the justice of the peace's office for some twenty minutes after learning that a lynch mob was on its way to the hospital. It was nearly nine o'clock when he left, strolling up Main Street toward the firehouse. At the corner of Second Avenue, he came upon Dr. Carmichael, police officers Robert Allison and Thomas Nafe and Burgess (mayor) Jesse Shallcross, who were engaged in a spirited conversation. Umsted joined the small crowd that had gathered around these prominent Coatesville citizens. Dr. Carmichael, seated in his automobile, was exhibiting the bullet he had removed from Walker's jaw and explaining the surgical procedure. However, once the police chief's presence was noted, the topic of discussion quickly changed to Walker's confession, and Umsted once again regaled those assembled with his comments. When Al Berry approached the group and tried to get Umsted's attention, the chief was immersed in his story and refused to notice. Berry, who had been searching frantically for the police (including two visits to the locked police station) ever since the lynch mob had moved down Main Street, now managed to pull Allison aside and tell him of the angry crowd's intention. The two men interrupted Umsted and told him what was happening; several other men chimed in that a crowd had already reached the hospital and was indeed going to lynch the prisoner. "I don't want to hear anything about it," Umsted shouted. He insisted that nothing was going to happen because the mob was just "a lot of hoodlums; they are a lot of young fellows and some of them don't know how to carry a gun. Why did they not lynch him this afternoon when they had him in the woods?" Frustrated by the chief's indifference, Berry got "hot under the collar" and told Umsted that he personally had prevented a lynching earlier in the day. "You are God damned popular for a man that has only been in town a few days," Umsted snapped. "You might be able to run a hot air balloon, but you cannot run me." Berry quickly retorted, "You have been warned about this…it is up to you to do your duty…I wash my hands of the whole matter." Then, livid with rage, he walked away. Umsted shouted after him, "No one asked you to butt in, in the first place."

Shortly after the shouting match subsided, the ambulance that had been searched at the hospital arrived back in Coatesville. Congestion along Strode Avenue had impeded its prompt return, so it was somewhat after the fact that Dr. Graves was able to report to the police chief that there was "trouble at the hospital" and that by now the lynch mob had surely had time to surround the building. He suggested that some police officers be sent to the hospital, arguing that even the sight of law authorities might deter the mob. Umsted replied that he had been up all of the night before and was tired. He also repeated his conviction that the people who had gathered at the hospital knew "what they would get if they made trouble" and that he "was not going to bother with them" since they intended no action. A few minutes later, he responded in the same manner to a telephone message sent by his superior, Richard Gibney, who insisted that the police were needed at the hospital. As chairman of the police committee, Gibney was extending to Umsted the authority to call out the sixteen fire policemen to serve as reinforcements. Umsted responded that he did not need to be told how to do his job. It was not until 9:15 p.m., after being summoned to the Stephenson House for an important telephone call—from an unidentified caller who reported that the mob at the hospital was threatening to remove Walker by force—that Umsted agreed to look into the situation. Dr. Carmichael volunteered the use of his automobile, and with Officer Allison they set out for the hospital.

The situation across town had clearly worsened. One witness recalled that the small hospital porch had "quite a few people" on it, probably about two dozen men and boys, while over two thousand onlookers filled the grounds and still more people could be seen on Strode Avenue. Confusion reigned supreme, both inside and outside the hospital. Someone in the crowd yelled out, "Don't let a nigger down a white man," prompting similar comments from those gathered on the lawn. Several people rang the hospital's entrance bell and pounded on the glass doors; some even tried to open the front doors, while others searched for different ways into the building. Obscenities were shouted out and threats were hurled at hospital staff members and patients alike. John Temple, the black orderly who had earlier been in Walker's room, and several nurses tried to calm terror-stricken patients (one of whom even fainted), while Miss Townsend pleaded through the glass doors with the crowd on the porch: "There are very sick people in this house, some at the point of death...go away." Her suggestion was greeted with a cascade of shouts and screams. Then someone on the porch tried to reason with her, saying, "Open up here; open up quietly and we will come in quietly, but we are going to get in or we are going to batter the doors down." Someone else added, "This dead officer is lying down there in Coatesville, and his family is left." The superintendent refused their demands and then retreated down a nearby corridor when several people began rattling the doors more violently. Officer Howe braced his burly six-foot, four-inch frame against the doors and called out to several people he thought he recognized in the crowd. He recalled later that all the time he was trying to persuade them to stop, they were "hollering and swearing and shoving and pushing."

At this point, those men on the porch began to engage in a dialogue of demands with the larger crowd. "We want more men," someone shouted. Another taunting voice rang out, "Would you stand down and see a black son of a bitch shoot one of your own men down? Are you all afraid, have you no sand?" Still another cried out for leadership: "We want somebody else up here, we want the man who knows." Several people called out for a man named Tucker to lead them. Someone in the crowd on the knoll shouted impatiently, "Come on, you got enough men up there to eat him," prompting the reply, "We have very few men; they are all boys." Again the cry went up for assistance on the porch: "Come on you sons of bitches, we can't do it ourselves. You ought to have more wit than to stand down and watch us."

As more men climbed onto the already crowded porch, Stanley Howe heard a familiar voice call out, "You might as well open the door, the mob is going to get him anyway." Then several people shouted in unison, "The negro or Howe!" and Howe stepped back, allowing the front doors to swing open. An unidentified man stepped inside, and when no one else on the porch followed him, he turned to them and beckoned, "Come on fellows, he is in here in a room by himself." Encouraged by this display of confidence, several people crossed the threshold, but once inside they were momentarily indecisive. One of them returned to the porch and challenged the mob, shouting, "Come on fellows, we can't do this ourselves. You are all cowards if you don't follow me." Suddenly, twelve to fifteen men stormed into the hospital "yelling like fiends."

Despite the close contact in the lighted hallway, neither Howe nor John Temple nor Miss Townsend claimed to recognize anyone in the crowd, perhaps because some (if not all) of the men wore handkerchiefs over their faces. Howe later stated, in defense of his conduct that night, that he had tried to hold back the crowd but that it "came pushing and shoving and hollering and screaming into the hallway" and easily brushed him aside. From a nearby closet, Temple observed that Howe had been "unable to check them or to offer any resistance." Temple added, "Not knowing what the excited crowd might do to me…when the mob approached my hiding place, I skedaddled to another part of the building." Amid the growing confusion, Miss Townsend and her small staff tried desperately to calm the frightened patients, several of whom attempted to leave the building.

Bursting into Walker's room, the angry mob descended on the hapless black man like vultures. As they began to pull at him, they discovered that he was straitjacketed to the bed and his leg was shackled to the post. Several people tore the straitjacket away while others looked for the keys to unlock the handcuffs. Officer Howe was brusquely shoved into the room, and "someone demanded the keys." When he informed them that only Chief Umsted had the keys, the men became livid. They tried to break the shackle but instead managed to tighten it around Walker's ankle, producing loud moans from the victim. Someone blurted out, "To Hell with the God-damn keys, we will tear the footboard off the bed"—which they did. Walker toppled to the floor and squirmed in obvious pain as blood soiled his bandages and spurted from his mouth. A man later identified as Tucker placed his hands on Howe's broad shoulders and advised him "to

The Coatesville Hospital, 1907, where Zachariah Walker was taken after his apprehension. *Courtesy of the Chester County Historical Society.*

offer no resistance." (Howe complied, as he stepped through the doorway of an adjacent room.) Then several people used the footboard of the bed as a handle and dragged the still conscious Walker down the main hospital corridor toward the front porch. His body partially suspended, Walker twisted and reeled in agony, prompting someone in the building to exclaim, "Watch the son of a bitch rolling now." The victim left "a trail of blood which flowed from his [head] wound."

The appearance of Zachariah Walker on the hospital porch brought a huge roar of approval from the crowd. His captors hesitated for a moment to acknowledge the cheers and then unceremoniously pulled him down the twenty-four porch steps. Amid jeers of "Shoot him!" "Burn him!" "Hang him!" he was dragged behind the footboard to the gate at the base of the knoll. Many in the throng shouted in unison, "Burn him, burn him!" while others took turns kicking and grabbing him or beating him with stones and sticks as he was dragged through an informal gauntlet. Walker's head, particularly his jaw, was a favorite target, not only because the blood-soaked bandages made an inviting target but also because a blow to the head produced more blood and excruciating screeches. Although Walker tried valiantly to protect himself, the blows were too numerous and too widely dispersed over his body. The mob leaders took sufficient interest in his condition to ensure that he was not rendered unconscious and therefore immune to further suffering.

Having reached the bottom of the hill, the mob hesitated and then stopped. One witness stated that the leaders "did not seem to know what to do or where to go." Several men called out again for Tucker to lead the way, but he refused to come down from the hospital porch. He gestured to the mob to continue without him and then entered the hospital to "pacify" the nurses and patients. All the while, chants of "Burn him," "Hang him," "Shoot him" continued. An unidentified man shouted over the crowd, "Take him up the road! Take him up to the woods," and on this advice another gauntlet was formed. Walker was being dragged farther into East Fallowfield Township (and beyond the jurisdiction of the Coatesville police force) when, at a bend in Towerville Road, those in the lead said they were "played out" and demanded that others share the burden. Fresh recruits took hold of the footboard, and the death march resumed.

As the mob made its way into the countryside beyond Coatesville, Police Chief Umsted, Officer Allison and Dr. Carmichael arrived at the hospital entrance. Several stragglers called out to them, "You are too late. They have taken him over the hill," but their shouts and gestures were ignored. Umsted and Carmichael left Allison at the gates to keep people off the grounds while they proceeded to the hospital building to confirm that a mob had in fact taken Walker away. Informed that the prisoner had been forcibly removed from the premises, Umsted chose not to pursue the mob but instead commenced a painstakingly detailed inspection of the hospital, which included the locks on the front doors and on Walker's room. He questioned Stanley Howe, John Temple and others, ascertaining how Walker had been abducted but not by whom. Then, despite the fact that Walker's agonizing screams and the crowd noise could be heard on the hospital lawn, Umsted and Carmichael rejoined Allison, and the three men returned to Coatesville. "Although informed by different persons that the mob had taken the prisoner up the hill," an official inquiry would conclude, "Umsted started in the opposite direction and made absolutely no effort to ascertain the fate of the negro or the identity of the persons who were murdering him."

Having dragged Walker for about a half mile, the men who were seemingly in charge stopped the procession near Sarah J. Newlin's farm. By now the angry crowd approached four thousand people, many of whom were screaming for the prisoner to die a slow, excruciatingly painful death; others wondered out loud why those at the front had stopped and shouted that something should be done. Finally, someone in the throng suggested that Walker be placed in the nearby Newlin barn and that they "burn barn and all." Jonas Newlin, who worked the farm and had been awakened by the noise, was mingling with the crowd when he realized what their intention was. He pushed to the front of the mob and successfully pleaded that the barn—his family's barn—be spared. An alternative course was quickly suggested: "Take him up in the field." Walker was then dragged about twenty feet off the public road, down a farm lane lined on both sides by a split-rail fence (which prevented the mob from taking him into the field). Once he was draped over the fence, the mob leaders determined, "with an almost inconceivably fiendish brutality," that he should be burned alive.

There was one practical problem to solve if Walker was to suffer such a fate: the recent rainstorms had soaked most of the available kindling, making it difficult to start a fire. Shouts of "Get straw, get straw" were heard, and several people ran to the Newlin barn and returned with armloads of hay and straw. With Walker still draped over the fence railing and still shackled to the footboard, the straw and hay were placed nearby and seven pieces of the fence railing were piled on top, along with what one observer recalled was a considerable amount of dampened firewood. The huge crowd spread out in an attempt to find the best possible vantage points for viewing the burning of Zachariah Walker. Some sat along the fence, while others clogged the lane; many others scurried to the open field or to an orchard that covered a nearby hill. After a suitable pyre was fashioned, a match was applied, and soon there was "a pretty good fire." The flickering light penetrated the dark August night, illuminating the faces of those closest to the flames. Many in the crowd edged closer, but the added commotion delayed the efforts to place more wood on the fire. Someone cried out, "Look out, let me through with this load of wood," and the crowd reluctantly parted.

As the fire grew, the men prepared to throw Walker on the pyre. "For God's sake, give a man a chance!" he begged. "I killed Rice in self-defense. Don't give me no crooked death because I'm not white!" But Walker's pleas fell upon deaf ears as the crowd answered with jeers, hoots and more cries of "Burn him, burn him!" The poor man was abruptly thrown into the fire, and in a matter of minutes the acrid smell of burnt hair and singed skin drifted in the night air. As Walker was enveloped in flames, a huge roar of approval went up from the crowd. One witness recalled that the "tongues of flame curled over the surface" of his body and "licked" at his skin, prompting Walker to let out several agonizing shrieks (which, it was

A view of the lynching site, with fence rails broken apart to stoke the fire. *Courtesy of the Chester County Historical Society.*

learned later, had been heard almost a mile away). Those close to the fire were bent forward, "eagerly watching the look of mingled horror and terror that distorted his blood-besmeared face." One teenage boy who had a good view of the proceedings remembered that "one side of him [was] pretty well burned and the skin was kind of hanging loose." It is no wonder that the crowd was surprised when Walker mustered the strength to crawl from the fire and onto the split-rail fence, his head touching the ground and his right foot still shackled to the footboard. After a moment's hesitation, several people scrambled forward to return the defiant victim to the inferno, and a teenage boy recalled that "somebody on the other side of the lane beat him over the head with a rail." Walker was either pushed with fence rails or was picked up and thrown back into the fire—no one seems to remember exactly how it happened—and his agonized screams again met with the approval of the crowd. Several fence rails, removed to prevent Walker from escaping again, were added to the fire or were used as clubs to beat him over the head while the flames continued to burn his flesh.

Somehow, Walker managed to crawl once more from the fire. The mob cheered this desperate act since it would serve to prolong the man's agony. Again he was clubbed over the head with fence rails and thrust back into the flames, strips of flesh hanging "from his already charred and blistered body." Summoning all of his energy, Walker emerged from the fire a third and final time, and those near the fire allowed him to crawl almost to their feet, admiring the "revolting spectacle his maimed and half-burned body presented to them." Finally, several men tied a rope around his neck and, holding onto both ends so that he could not escape, pulled him back into the fire. Walker gave one last terrible shriek and fell back, "while the flames shot higher and higher." In the words of one observer, his pyre was now "an indistinguishable sheet of fire." Death ended Zachariah Walker's unimaginable agony at about 9:30 p.m., little more than a half hour after he was dragged from his hospital bed. Thousands of eyes gazed intently into the fire, and as "men and boys danced and capered in the moonlight," the leaders of the mob retreated into the welcoming darkness of the night. Within an hour, the crowd had dwindled, and only the occasional spit or crack from the rain-soaked wood could be heard over their murmurings.

As the majority of the crowd slowly, almost reluctantly, departed the lynching site, *Coatesville Record* reporter H.E. Williams told a companion, "This will be an awful lesson to some of the niggers who came from the South, but it is a damned shame that they took this man from the hospital after the law had him." His friend offered no argument. There was a moment's panic when car lights were seen coming from the hospital and someone hollered, "Look out, here come the cops in an automobile." Suddenly wary of their actions, many people fled. But it was only a carload of curious Coatesville residents, "not the cops." In fact, the police did not visit the scene of Walker's death that night. Among those who watched the departing crowd was a group of teenage boys who had been quite close to the fire during Walker's ordeal. They were loudly expressing their approval of the spectacle and could not help but agree with a man leaning against the fence who exclaimed, "By God, boys, we made a clean job of it!" One of them suggested that they all go to the Coatesville Candy Company, since this was something of "an holiday occasion," and get a cold soda to satisfy their thirst while they discussed the evening's events. As they set off, the

Zachariah Walker's remains, which fit into a shoe box. The photograph was taken by court photographer Joseph Belt the morning after the lynching. *Courtesy of the Chester County Historical Society.*

town clock struck ten. After two drinks apiece, the boys went home, for Monday was a workday.

One newspaper reported that "five thousand men, women and children [had] stood by and watched the proceedings as though it were a ball game or another variety of outdoor sport." The *Coatesville Record* noted the politeness of the crowd, with men stepping aside to allow women and children a better view of the burning. Other newspapers stated that there had been as many women in the mob as men and that not a single voice had been raised that night in protest. Approximately 150 individuals maintained an all-night vigil near the fire, waiting to collect souvenirs. Some of the more aggressive among them used fence railings to dredge Walker's bones from the glowing embers. The manacles and footboard were also pulled from the pyre and then doused in water and broken up as souvenirs. The next day, several enterprising boys even sold some of Walker's remains to anxious customers in Coatesville. A curious reporter who visited the lynching site several months later found many changes, including the absence of grass where the burning took place and the almost complete demolition of the split-rail fence. "Visitors have carried away anything that looked like a souvenir," he wrote.

On Monday morning, Mrs. Annie Rice, widow of the dead policeman, indicated her satisfaction with the events of the previous evening. She admitted to reporters that she had "begged" to accompany the mob but that several men had insisted she remain at home. "I would have done anything to have got near him [Walker], but they would not let me," she declared. "I wanted to apply the match. I wanted to see him burn." When told of Walker's demise, Widow Rice expressed no remorse. In her opinion, "He got just what he deserved."

Chapter 2

"A Conspiracy of Silence"

E dgar Rice was a special policeman of the Borough of Coatesville, humane and fearless. Zachariah Walker was a worthless negro from Virginia." So began the reminiscences of Wilmer W. MacElree, one of Chester County's most prominent and respected trial attorneys. MacElree likely spoke for many of the residents of Coatesville and the surrounding county. The tragic events of August 12–13, 1911, brought Coatesville to the attention of the nation and the world. Inhabitants of this middling industrial town soon found themselves exposed to tremendous scrutiny and scorn. Faced with such continuous attention over a period of nearly a year, harangued by hostile voices both near and far, they withdrew into what a grand jury described as "a conspiracy of silence." Their intent was to protect the borough's reputation as well as the identity of those who were directly involved in Walker's death. At the center of the local campaign to dissociate Coatesville from the lynching was the town's major newspaper, the *Coatesville Record*. Through its coverage of events and its daily commentary, the *Record* helped to shape public opinion and popular perceptions of what actually had occurred that Sunday evening.

Like the residents of Coatesville, the *Record* and its editor, William Long, proved to be extremely sensitive to all forms of criticism. Not surprisingly, as the chief defender of the community's honor, the paper argued for a particular understanding of events even as interested parties outside the borough came to view the incident in a far more incriminating light. One early indication that the *Record* would not be an impartial observer was the damning pronouncement on Monday, August 14, that the "most awful crime in the history of Coatesville" was the murder of Edgar Rice, not the lynching of Zachariah Walker. The newspaper informed its readers that Walker had murdered Rice "in cold blood" while the popular Worth Brothers police officer was on duty. It reminded them that Rice had, until a year ago, been a loyal, popular member of the borough police force and had nearly been elected chief of police. Walker was described as "a floating negro" who had come to Coatesville in recent months to work in the mills. He was an outsider, and drunk at the time of the altercation, whereas Rice was the epitome of an insider, raised on a nearby farm and for years a respected member of the community. No mention was made of Walker's claim that he had killed Rice in self-defense.

An interesting feature of that first report in the *Record* was the conclusion regarding who actually participated in the lynching. The clear impression given was that the mob leaders were at present unknown and would probably never be known to authorities. For all of its exhaustive coverage, the paper

A crowd of curious townsfolk assembles at the lynching site the next morning. Image taken by court photographer Joseph Belt. *Courtesy of the Chester County Historical Society.*

failed to reveal the identity of a single eyewitness, either at the hospital or at the site of the lynching; in fact, it claimed that the mob leaders all wore masks to shield their faces from recognition. Then, apparently contradicting itself, the *Record* stated: "It has been said on the streets that there were several Southern people, strangers in town last night, and there were strange faces in front of the mob who dragged the negro from the hospital." The implication was obvious. Outsiders—*southerners*, of course—having learned of Rice's death, entered Coatesville on Sunday looking to cause trouble, and *they* were the ones who killed Walker and then fled into the enveloping darkness of night, never to return. Furthermore, as the paper argued the next day, the lynching did not occur within the borough, and Coatesville thus could not be held responsible "for what was done outside her borders in the heat of inhuman frenzy." Such behavior would be out of character, for "the general temper of the people of Coatesville is peace-loving and law-abiding."

Even as word spread that the district attorney had the names of persons seen in the crowd, the *Record* held to its explanation of events and to its conviction that the facts were sufficient to absolve the town and its residents of any blame. Most of the community had confidence in the newspaper's representation of what had occurred and who was at fault. Yet in time, a different story began to emerge. The editorial comments of major metropolitan newspapers and periodicals around the state and across the nation were more critical (and at times contained erroneous information and bold misstatements of fact). In nearby Philadelphia, the *Inquirer* and the *Bulletin* carried scathing indictments. In New York, the *Times* stated bluntly that "nowhere in the United States was a man ever lynched with less excuse or with an equal heaping up of horror on horror." These sentiments were echoed in the *World*, the *Herald* and the *Evening Post*. In Chicago, both the *Tribune* and the *Daily News* offered similar judgments, and elsewhere in the North newspaper editors agreed with the *Outlook*'s assessment that Coatesville was "A BLOT ON CIVILIZATION."

The harshest attacks on the residents of Coatesville came from West Chester, a longtime rival in county politics. Whereas Coatesville was the largest municipality in Chester County and contributed more revenues to the county treasury, West Chester was the seat of governance. The *Coatesville Record*'s editor countered the criticism of West Chester's *Daily Local News* by pointing out that West Chester had ulterior motives in rebuking Coatesville. In more than one editorial over a period of several months, Long argued that the West Chester crowd was simply trying to reap political gain by embarrassing the borough and that the severe treatment amounted to nothing more than politics as usual, albeit West Chester style.

Newspapers in most Pennsylvania steel towns tended to downplay the happenings in Coatesville, either by giving no coverage to the lynching or by relegating it to the back pages. The weekly *Steelton Press*, published outside of Harrisburg, printed its first and only article on the affair on September 16, even though it carried numerous articles in August and September detailing violent crimes committed elsewhere in Pennsylvania. The *Johnstown Weekly Democrat*, which reported regularly on the lynching, presented Walker in an unflattering light, dubbing him a "negro desperado." According to the *Democrat*, "That the burning of the negro was designed and carried out by level-headed men there can be no doubt." It was, the paper declared, the work of men "ready to take any kind of chance to avenge the death of the respectable citizen who had been shot down in cold blood."

Throughout the South, editors observed that racial lynching was not peculiar to one region of the country. In its August 15 editorial, "Northern Pot and Southern Kettle," the *Washington Post* posed this question: "It may seem a reversion of time honored methods but what is wrong with the suggestion that a few Southern missionaries be sent northward to teach their benighted brethren the principles of right-doing in the much mooted race question?" That same day, the Richmond (Virginia) *Times* noted with words that proved to be prophetic, "The mob which was strong enough to defy the law will be strong enough to defeat the law."

Long after other publications had forgotten about the lynching of Zachariah Walker, African American newspapers and journals continued to report on developments in the case. Among the more than one dozen journals that carried periodic updates were the *Chicago Defender*, the *Washington Bee*, the *Indianapolis Freeman* and the *Pittsburgh Courier*. In the *Boston Guardian*, perhaps the most outspoken of all African American publications, Monroe Trotter printed a terse commentary under the banner "Coatesville—Its Lessons." What happened in Pennsylvania was not peculiar to one community or state, he reasoned, but rather was symptomatic of the evils of American society as a whole. T. Thomas Fortune, writing in the *New York Age*, echoed Trotter's outrage: "Nothing in Central Africa could have equaled it. Nothing that has occurred in Haiti in its darkest days will compare with this atrocious and barbaric display."

"A Conspiracy of Silence"

For the fledgling National Association for the Advancement of Colored People (NAACP), established in 1910 to combat lynching and other racial injustices, the events in Coatesville took on greater significance than any other lynching to date. The NAACP national office sent telegrams to Governor John K. Tener, State Police Superintendent John Groome and Coatesville's chief executive, Burgess Jesse Shallcross, calling for the swift arrest and prosecution of all those involved in the deplorable murder. For the next nine months, the organization's monthly magazine, *The Crisis*, monitored the situation in Coatesville, bringing the latest information to the attention of the African American community and to a substantial number of white readers as well. The September 1911 issue, for example, presented a summary of negative editorial comments from a half-dozen prominent newspapers, along with a response from Coatesville's mayor to the telegram he had received: "We are certainly using every effort to bring the perpetrators of the outrageous act of burning a human being while still alive...notwithstanding what may be said by those outside it will develop that the guilty ones will be found and punished to the full extent of the law... We are striving to redeem ourselves, which the future will prove."

"Let the eagle scream!" W.E.B. Du Bois proclaimed in an editorial in that same issue sarcastically titled "Triumph." "Again the burden of upholding the best traditions of Anglo-Saxon civilization has fallen on the sturdy shoulders of the American republic." He placed much significance on the fact that Walker was lynched on a Sunday evening and that, according to numerous reports, the churches had emptied as word of the impending deed spread. "Ah, the splendor of that Sunday night dance...Let the eagle scream! / Civilization is again safe." He continued: "Some foolish people talk of punishing the heroic mob, and the Governor of Pennsylvania seems to be real provoked. There may be a few arrests, but the men will be promptly released by the mob sitting as jury—perhaps even as judge. America knows her true heroes. Again, let the eagle scream!"

Although the African American press excoriated Coatesville, the black community within the borough was remarkably restrained in its reaction to the lynching. There were newspaper accounts that unidentified local blacks had sought revenge for Rice's murder by joining the lynch mob, with one man allegedly saying of Walker, "Let me at him! I'll cut his d--- heart out." However, there is little evidence that the native black community of Coatesville had felt any special kinship with Walker. Five days after the lynching, a group

A view of downtown Coatesville looking west from Second Avenue. Pollution from the steel mills clouds the air. *Courtesy of the Frank Pennegar Collection and the Chester County Historical Society.*

of ten prominent black citizens did sign a memorial protesting his death, but they were careful to condemn both murders; and while criticizing the practice of lynching in general, they exercised caution in calling for the prosecution of the instigators. No one, including this group of respected ministers, businessmen and professionals, was prepared to rush to Walker's defense, but as matters stood in Coatesville in the summer of 1911, it is not surprising that they did not issue a stronger statement on the lynching.

There was an uneasy calm in Coatesville in the days following the lynching. The "more sober-minded men" of the town cautioned restraint, as rumors of investigations and arrests circulated, while the *Record* allowed that the citizens of Coatesville did not want "hasty action" on the matter. One lifelong resident, who recalled the incident years later, said that most of the prominent leaders in the community were acutely embarrassed by the episode but felt powerless to correct the wrong after the fact. A concerted effort was made to return to normalcy—or at least to give the appearance of normalcy. The lynching had occurred in the middle of the summer picnic season, which coincided with the end of the annual Harvest Home Festival celebrating the blessings of community life. On Monday, August 14, the Business Men's Association announced that its annual picnic would take place as planned, and two days later more than one thousand people journeyed some thirty miles by train and automobile to a park near Reading. The men's Industrial League baseball schedule, a matter of great local concern, continued undisturbed. Several Coatesville teams had a chance to make the playoffs, and the townspeople were excited by the prospects of a championship. Mid-August was also the time when local clergy went on their vacations, and by one account, seven of the eight Christian ministers in Coatesville were out of town the week following the lynching.

Aware that criticism of Coatesville was spreading rapidly, Burgess Shallcross called a special meeting of the borough council for Monday afternoon, August 14. The purpose of the meeting, which convened just as a special issue of the *Record* hit the streets, was to "take some action

Corey Park athletic field and the Viaduct Mill, Coatesville, circa 1911. The lynch mob crossed this open space on its way to the hospital. *Courtesy of the Chester County Historical Society.*

concerning the burning of Zach S. Walker on Sunday the 13th." In the course of preliminary discussions, Councilman H.B. Spackman, a respected businessman, suggested that the council could do no more than condemn both the Walker and Rice murders since they had occurred outside the borough. His comment prompted considerable debate, which went unrecorded in the official minutes but was reported in detail in the West Chester paper. Richard Gibney, the councilman who had challenged Chief Umsted to act during the crisis, eventually introduced a compromise motion, which passed without dissent:

> *Whereas a series of dastardly crimes have* [been] *committed contiguous to and adjoining Coatesville, in the murder of Edgar Rice Saturday night, Aug 12 by Zachariah S. Walker and the subsequent events of taking Walker from the Coatesville Hospital in Valley Township and the brutal murder of Walker in East Fallowfield Township on Sunday evening Aug 13…*
>
> *And while we deplore and regret the report published broadcast holding our Borough responsible for this crime…*
>
> *We Resolve that the Burgess and Town Council of Coatesville hereby condemn the brutal murder of Edgar Rice and the mob violence of entering a hospital and the outrageous barbarism and cruel action of the murder of Zach S. Walker.*
>
> *And we further Resolve that the authorities of Coatesville cooperate with the county and state, offering every assistance possible toward apprehension and conviction of those persons guilty of this outrage.*

The resolution seemed to blame both sides at once, but while the council's condemnation of the lynching appeared sincere, the members made it clear that they considered the crimes to have occurred outside their jurisdiction. Technically, Rice *had* been killed beyond the southern boundary of the borough, and Walker *had* been abducted from a hospital that stood just outside the borough limits, and the lynching *had* taken place a half mile outside of town in East Fallowfield Township. So in the minds of council members and the burgess, Coatesville was absolved from responsibility. It may have been a mistake to have kept Walker in the Coatesville Hospital rather than transport him immediately to West Chester, some people argued, but that error in judgment did not change the facts. Thus, after approving

Gibney's resolution, the council adjourned until its next regular meeting in September. There is no record that the borough council ever again formally discussed the circumstances of Zachariah Walker's death.

The borough council had attempted to deflect blame from Coatesville, and many residents joined in the hope that the storm of controversy would soon blow over. But county and state officials were of a different mind. Like most states, Pennsylvania had no antilynching law in 1911, but murder was a capital offense. Within twenty-four hours of Walker's death, District Attorney Gawthrop announced that there would be a full investigation into the incident and that those proven to be culpable would be prosecuted. "We will clear this thing up if it takes ten years to do it," he told the *Coatesville Record* on Monday. A prominent West Chester attorney and leader of the county Republican Party, Robert Gawthrop was nearing the end of his tenure as district attorney. He was also embroiled in a highly publicized libel suit against William Long and the *Record*, a matter that served to complicate his relationship with the newspaper as the lynching investigation developed. Although his legal skills were highly regarded, as was his prowess on the tennis court and at the bridge table, his steadfast resolve to see justice done in the Walker murder put him at odds with most of the residents of Coatesville and with much of Chester County. Assisted by Harris Sproat, Gawthrop pursued his inquiry for nine months, but in the end he found that his greatest obstacle was the attitude of the very people who had several times elected him chief county prosecutor.

Pennsylvania Governor John K. Tener, who was in New York when the lynching occurred, issued a statement that the commonwealth would spare no expense to bring the leaders of the mob to justice. Tener, a native of Ireland, had won fame as a professional baseball player and member of Albert Spalding's celebrated 1888 world tour. Then, after a brief career in banking in western Pennsylvania, he had entered state politics and was elected governor in 1910. Tener was sincere in his belief that the Coatesville lynching represented an unparalleled challenge to decency and democracy in Pennsylvania, although one resident of the town recalled that certain civic leaders shared W.E.B. Du Bois's doubts about the governor's resolve. Some people apparently considered his statements to be all sound and fury—nothing more than public posturing for personal gain.

In the days following the incident, Tener ordered State Attorney General John C. Bell and his deputy, Jesse B. Cunningham, to assist local authorities in the investigation. He also instructed State Police Superintendent John Groome to cooperate in any way possible. Although there was little evidence to warrant such a concern, the sheriff of Chester County feared that a race riot was imminent in Coatesville and, with Gawthrop's consent, requested the assistance of the state constabulary. Late on Monday evening, August 14, a detachment of seventeen state policemen from Pottsville and Malvern arrived in Coatesville by special train. After conferring with Charles Umsted, the local police chief, they began patrolling every neighborhood in the borough. The men of Troop C found two things to be obvious from the moment they arrived: first, "everything was quiet" and expectations of racial unrest were unfounded; and second, the citizens of Coatesville did not appreciate the presence of outside law enforcement officers. As the days passed, this resentment only hardened, making the work of the investigators all the more difficult. Under the circumstances, it is therefore not surprising that the combined efforts of county and state officials led to the most expensive criminal investigation in the history of the Commonwealth of Pennsylvania up to that time.

For fifteen days, the state police patrolled Coatesville's streets, assisting in the investigation and ready to handle any disturbances. The sight of a battalion of mounted policemen along Chestnut Street near the borough hall infuriated some local residents. At the request of Gawthrop, Coatesville saloons restricted their hours for several weeks in an effort to prevent public fighting, which led to complaints by tavern owners that the decreased public consumption of liquor and beer was hurting business. Of course, people were staying away from the bars not so much because of the curfew but because citizens feared that if certain folks drank too much, they might start talking about what they had seen on the evening of August 13. It was widely rumored— and later substantiated—that undercover agents were in town and that they were frequenting the saloons in an effort to obtain information. These agents were not the Pinkerton detectives who initially were working in cooperation with the state police but rather four patrolmen from Troop C who remained behind after the others left Coatesville, their true identities carefully protected by local authorities. These plainclothes officers were, in fact, instrumental in obtaining leads that brought about the arrest of seven men.

Unsubstantiated rumors abounded as the investigation proceeded, with perhaps the greatest number of them involving the background of Zachariah Walker. The *Coatesville Record* carried a story about a group of unnamed black men from Walker's home county in Virginia who now resided in Bernardtown and knew Walker to be a "bad negro." There was a report that an unidentified Polish youth from the Spruces claimed that he had actually seen Walker shoot Rice. Still another story involved a boy named Henry Yesacavitz who told a reporter that Rice had been in the Spruces early Saturday evening and had questioned Walker about stealing some chickens—the implication being that when the two men met later that evening on the Youngsburg Road, Rice already knew Walker as a criminal type. Although Yesacavitz was never heard from again, and no one with that name was ever questioned by investigators, this and other dubious stories in the local paper served to cast Walker in an increasingly undesirable light. Meanwhile, from West Chester came fresh rumors that Police Chief Umsted had the names of men allegedly involved in the lynching and that some of the men were ready to name names. It was also said that the county sheriff had identified eighteen witnesses within thirty-six hours of the crime, but when they were questioned on Tuesday, August 15, none claimed to know of anyone who had a hand in the lynching. The next day, the *Philadelphia Inquirer* reported that five men had come forward and confessed their involvement in the lynching; a few days later, it speculated that the entire Coatesville police force, including its two black officers, was about to be arrested for complicity in the lynching. All of these tales proved to be entirely without foundation.

On August 16, as preparations were being made for Edgar Rice's funeral, the *Record* reported that Kennedy Boyd, a thirty-year-old electric light lineman, had been arrested the previous evening and had confessed his role in the lynching. It was said that he had given the police additional names and that other arrests were expected to follow quickly. This appeared to be the first big break in the case. However, in an adjacent column was an article whose contents directly rebutted the charges against Boyd. Fellow residents of his boardinghouse vouched for Boyd's decency and claimed that he could not have been involved in the abduction and lynching as he was sitting with them on the front porch Sunday evening when the great crowd went by toward the hospital. Only after the throng had passed did he leave his chair and start out after it. Therefore, if anything, he was but an innocent bystander, like so many others. The next day, the paper reported that Boyd had been released after questioning.

Thursday, August 17, was a day of great catharsis for the residents of Coatesville. That morning, Edgar Rice was laid to rest in the shadows of the tasteful Gothic façade of the Hephzibah Baptist Church near Youngsburg. The funeral was remembered as the largest and most emotional in the history of Coatesville, with an estimated six thousand people accompanying the cortege the several miles from Rice's home to the hillside cemetery. On their march, the mourners crossed the bridge over the Brandywine Creek, at the very spot where Rice had lost his life. In addition to members of the Rice family, trustees of the Brandywine Fire Company attended the casket. Observers remarked on the unprecedented outpouring of sympathy for Widow Rice and her children. Rice was eulogized for his decency and courage, a martyr who had surrendered his life in the line of duty. He might be gone from their midst, but no one believed he would soon be forgotten.

Before the funeral service concluded, officials announced in town that additional arrests had been made the previous evening. Residents were shocked to learn that three people—all local men—had been brought before Squire S.M. Paxson in West Chester and charged with murder. Joseph Schofield was forty years old and an employee of the trolley company. Until three years earlier, he had lived in Coatesville; now he resided with his wife and children west of the borough near Parkesburg. Norman Price was a native son, raised on a farm in nearby Caln Township, and like Walker he was employed at the Worth Brothers mill. The third person arrested was fifteen-year-old George Stoll. The son of the police chief in Marietta, Pennsylvania, some forty-five miles west of Coatesville, Stoll lived in Coatesville at the home of his sister and brother-in-law and worked as a crane operator for the Coatesville Foundry and Machine Company.

The evidence linking the three to the lynching was as varied as their identities. Schofield was alleged to have been at the forefront of the mob that Sunday evening; he was also accused of being one of the masked men who abducted Walker from the hospital. Price apparently confessed to taking part in the lynching, at least to the extent that he admitted entering the hospital, but he protested that he was not one of the leaders. Stoll was not so timid as Price when questioned by the police. The *Record* claimed that county officials had evidence the teenager was in fact one of the leaders and that he was heard to have bragged to friends that it would "be a cinch" to get Walker out of the hospital. Stoll "displayed the most wonderful nerve" during his interrogation, the newspaper reported. A county official commented, "His nerves are as hard as iron. He is the most stubborn boy I ever saw." District Attorney Gawthrop seemed pleased with the early arrests and confident that the evidence gathered so far would lead to the identification of other principals in the crime. His confidence was short-lived, however, as local resistance to the inquiry gained strength with each passing day.

On Friday, August 18, the citizens of Coatesville were again shaken from a belief that outsiders were responsible for Walker's death when authorities detained five other local men. Chester Bostic, nineteen years old and, like Stoll, a native of Marietta, was arrested and charged with murder, rioting and inciting to riot. Bostic was employed at the Lukens Iron and Steel Company and boarded at the home of Mrs. Anna Scott on Chestnut Street; he was known as a quiet lad who kept to himself. Mrs. Scott was clearly dismayed when informed of her tenant's predicament. "Chester was a nice boy, a very nice boy," she responded when asked about his character. The *Coatesville Record* remarked that county officials were satisfied that Bostic, who was held without bail, was among the leaders on that fateful Sunday night.

The other men detained that day were each held on $1,000 bail as material witnesses. Richard Tucker, a prominent insurance agent with the Prudential Company, a longtime member of the Brandywine Fire Company and a resident of the borough for more than ten years, had been a close friend of Edgar Rice. William Gilbert was a local railroad engineer, and Dale Hadley

Members of the Coatesville Brandywine Fire Company, circa 1911. *Courtesy of the Frank Pennegar Collection and the Chester County Historical Society.*

was a "hokey-pokey" (ice cream) vendor. Albert Berry, of Philadelphia, who had helped capture Walker, was the fourth person taken into custody. Only Tucker and Hadley made bail; the others spent the weekend in jail. Gawthrop believed that all four men possessed information vital to his investigation, and in its Saturday edition the *Record* echoed that sentiment. It further stated that officials were confident at least two of the eight people detained since Wednesday were involved in the hospital abduction.

Late Saturday afternoon, a ninth man was arrested and charged with murder. Joseph Swartz, a nineteen-year-old from Phoenixville (northeast of Coatesville), allegedly confessed that he had taken part in the abduction and killing of Walker. While reporting on the newest development in the case, the *Record* took the occasion to recount the gruesome details of the lynching, including the young man's admission that he had gathered hay for the fire. The district attorney also issued a statement in which he accused Gilbert and Berry of having taken part in the crime.

Despite considerable progress in the investigation, a great deal of confusion remained over what had actually happened on the evening of August 13. Charges and countercharges were leveled by some of the accused, and erroneous and misleading statements circulated freely throughout Chester County. It was also apparent that authorities were having great difficulty getting anyone to talk openly, and no grand jury had been called to consider formal indictments. On Monday, August 21, the coroner's report was released, but it contained no startling revelations. Based on Dr. Carmichael's "internal examination" of both corpses, Dr. William McKinley concluded that Edgar Rice's death had been caused by a "gun shot wound by the hands of Zachariah Walker…while said Edgar Rice was in the performance of his official duty as an officer of the law." Walker had died in East Fallowfield Township by "being burned to Death on a fire by persons unknown to the [coroner's] jury." Five witnesses had been called regarding the manner of Rice's death; none had been called on behalf of Walker. Chief Umsted announced that same day that, given existing ambiguities and delays in the inquiry, as well as the need to interview additional witnesses, the entire matter might not come before the county court in its October session. The state's case, it seems, was far from secure.

On Tuesday morning, there was high drama in the Chester County Courthouse in West Chester. J. Paul MacElree, the attorney retained by George Stoll, requested that his client either be formally charged or released

Judge William Butler, the West Chester magistrate who presided over several of the lynching trials. Butler had strong words for juries who failed to convict several of the accused. *Courtesy of the Chester County Historical Society.*

on the grounds of habeas corpus—in this case, insufficient evidence to warrant confinement. Judge William Butler of the Court of Oyer and Terminer then listened to several witnesses who placed Stoll at the hospital and at the scene of the lynching. Among them was Police Officer Stanley Howe, who not only identified Stoll as one of the people on the hospital porch that night but also quoted Stoll as saying, "You might as well open the door, as we'll get him anyhow." Two other witnesses told the judge that Stoll had indeed been present at the lynching, though they could not say whether he had taken an active part in the burning. MacElree called such testimony ambiguous and requested that his client be released on bail since no one had accused him of actually holding the torch that ignited the pyre. But the judge concluded that there was sufficient cause to hold the teenager on the charge of murder, pending the findings of a grand jury, and therefore denied MacElree's request. He also took the opportunity to express his personal belief that those who sanctioned the actions of the crowd, those who stood by and did nothing to prevent the lynching, were accomplices to murder.

Butler's comments served as a bold challenge to the community, which thus far had refused to cooperate in the investigation. In the days that followed, newspapers in several states reprinted the judge's remarks, and he began to receive numerous letters that praised him for his stand, lauding his "masterful courage" and "kindness for the colored race." From New York, the noted minister and social reformer Dr. C.H. Parkhurst wrote to congratulate Butler, reminding the jurist that "the country is watching you." The district attorney was encouraged by Butler's statement and pledged to broaden his investigation to include sympathizers as well as leaders of the mob. "We are going to arrest everyone who was in that crowd that went from Coatesville to the hospital and followed the lynchers when they carried Walker down over the hospital lawn and were around the fire when he was burned," Gawthrop announced on Tuesday afternoon.

True to his word, by that evening Gawthrop had two more men in custody. Little was known of Herbert Smith, whom the *Record* called a "mystery," except that he was from Philadelphia and had been seen at the lynching site. Eighteen-year-old Clyde Woodward, on the other hand, was from Coatesville and, like Walker and several of the accused, worked at Worth Brothers. James Hughes, a co-worker, said, "Woodward is just one of those big, long-legged boys who are full of fun. I don't think he ever went with that mob with the intention of doing anyone any harm. He simply went along to see what was going on; he wouldn't be a boy if he didn't." Apparently, the authorities agreed with Hughes's assessment because both Woodward and Smith were cleared of any wrongdoing and released after a brief interrogation.

On Wednesday, August 23, perhaps the most damning criticism of Coatesville to appear in print was carried in the *Record*. The criticism came from a Swarthmore, Pennsylvania man who wrote for the Chicago religious publication the *Continent*. Under the banner *"Civilization's Failure at Coatesville,"* William Ellis castigated every segment of the community for not only failing to stop the lynching but for being unwilling to bring the guilty parties to justice. Ellis explained that he had arrived in Coatesville on August 15 and was appalled to discover that, just forty-eight hours after the lynching, local ministers were out of town on vacation and the Catholic priest was away visiting a sick brother. "In the hour of trial they all failed," he wrote. The townspeople seemed unconcerned, with the best citizens adopting an attitude of "leave us alone" and a hope that the "thing" would blow over. "No good citizen came out with an appeal to conscience," Ellis claimed. "Coatesville had no voice, no vocal conscience, apparently no sense of guilt." He then continued with great rhetorical flair: "Unless the white light and heat of a nation's blazing indignation be concentrated on Coatesville, it is extremely improbable that any adequate punishment will be meted out."

As if such strong comments were not enough to elicit the wrath of most residents, Ellis presented an altogether different scenario of Rice's fatal confrontation with Walker. Based on sources he would not disclose, and offering no evidence to substantiate his theory, Ellis wrote that it was possible the policeman had also been under the influence of alcohol when he met Walker on the darkened road. What followed was a drunken brawl during which Walker killed Rice in self-defense, just as he had claimed in his confession. But where intemperance may have provoked the confrontation, Ellis continued, it was irreligion that explained the community's inability to come to terms with the crisis. As in so many other small towns across the country, it all boiled down to a failure of character, a failure of religion: "In a word, it was a social, political, moral and religious collapse on the part of the community that is no worse than most of its neighbors, and better than some." According to Ellis, the crime of August 13 exposed a fundamental flaw in the "present-day American character" in which cheap sensations and irreligion are allowed to rule. "I do not rail at this respectable, prosperous, commonplace old Pennsylvania town," he explained. "I regard it as merely 'Exhibit A' in a study of American life."

Although the *Record* was clearly not in agreement with Ellis's remarks, citing them as another example of outside interference, it printed the article in an attempt to be fair-minded. As might be expected, residents of Coatesville took little comfort in this assessment of their moral condition, for everything Ellis said countered the image civic leaders had labored for years to build. They did not think of themselves as "small-souled politicians first and executors of the law afterward"; nor did they consider themselves an especially provincial, non-churchgoing folk who engaged in corner loafing and held a "lust for new sensations." Several days after the piece ran in the newspaper, Burgess Jesse Shallcross announced that he was suing Ellis for libel. Among other things, Shallcross did not appreciate being called a "doddering and fatuous old burgess." When informed of Shallcross's intentions, Ellis responded: "This suit is in itself a trifle, but it may result in an important contribution to the vindication of Pennsylvania and the cause of justice." However, aside from a bit of comic relief, the suit had little effect on affairs in Coatesville or elsewhere in the state.

In the midst of the flap over the Ellis article, authorities arrested another man and charged him with being an accessory to murder. Based on information reportedly given by Norman Price, thirty-four-year-old Oscar Lamping, a resident of the borough, was accused of agitating the crowd that had gathered on Main Street to lynch Walker. In acknowledging Lamping's arrest, the district attorney remarked, "We got the stuff on this man."

On Saturday, August 26, the eight men who were being held on charges of murder—Joseph Swartz, Joseph Schofield, George Stoll, Norman Price, Chester Bostic, William Gilbert, Albert Berry and Oscar Lamping—were given a hearing before Squire Paxson in West Chester. At this point in the investigation, Price and Bostic were cooperating with officials, though neither had been promised immunity from prosecution. For two and a half hours, Paxson heard testimony from a variety of witnesses regarding each of the accused. Three of the men—Gilbert, Berry and Swartz—were placed at the scene of the abduction; the others were identified as having been at the scene of the lynching. But none of the witnesses testified that any of these men had actually participated in the burning of Zachariah Walker. In fact, authorities had yet to uncover hard evidence linking anyone to the actual murder. After the hearing, all eight men were taken back to the West Chester jail amid rumors that Oscar Lamping had tried to kill himself.

As the second week of the investigation drew to a close, officials in West Chester were confident that the information they possessed was adequate to secure indictments against the eight men now in custody. On Monday, August 28, two weeks after they had arrived, the detachment of state police turned over what information they had gathered to District Attorney Gawthrop and returned to their regular patrols. On Tuesday, Judge Butler addressed members of a county grand jury in the matter of the lynching and the charges against the accused. It was expected that within the week the grand jury would begin its independent inquiry—an unwelcome development as far as residents of Coatesville and much of Chester County were concerned. "If the informal information we possess is accurate," Gawthrop told the jury, "never has [a] more fiendish, cowardly crime been committed; never has the law more wantonly and recklessly been defied." He continued:

> *We have been accustomed to look upon lynchings in the South as inexplicable acts of inhuman brutality far removed from us, and not possible to be contemplated, much less to be executed by those living in our midst.*

Now, not only in our state but in our county has this abominable crime been perpetrated, and for the first time are we viewed with horror, have we real cause to feel shamed and disgraced.

Apparently not one extenuating circumstance was present to modify to the slightest degree the aspect of devilish depraved wickedness, of contemptible cowardice...with details sickening and horrible beyond portrayal, conceivable only with veritable, benighted savages, they proceeded to, and did destroy this human being on Sunday evening, about the time the people were returning from their churches.

Toward the end of his address, Gawthrop presented a powerful characterization of Walker's killers: "Men who took part were more cowardly than wolves, and more devilish than fiends when they tortured the man as they did."

On Friday, September 1, the grand jury was impaneled in West Chester. The jury was made up chiefly of farmers and small businessmen from the county, with one member from Coatesville and two others from neighboring East Fallowfield Township. One by one the defendants were called in, along with Police Chief Umsted and Officer Howe. A crowd of reporters, friends of the accused and curious onlookers filled the main corridor of the courthouse and made passage to and from its chambers difficult. Coatesville residents who mingled in the hallway wished Norman Price and Chester Bostic well. To nearly everyone's surprise, it took only a few hours for the jury to vote true bills of indictment on charges of murder and instigating a riot against all eight men. An obviously pleased Robert Gawthrop announced that the defendants would stand trial in the October session of the court and that Attorney General John C. Bell and his deputy, J.E.B. Cunningham, would represent the commonwealth in the prosecutions.

In Coatesville, word of the indictments brought a mixed reaction, as did word that the grand jury would resume its inquiry on Monday morning. On Saturday, the *Record* attempted to downplay the significance of the grand jury action, although it admitted that thirty-two witnesses had been called for Monday. The *Record* maintained:

So far as can be gathered from the stray remarks of the jurors, their opinions and convictions seem to coincide exactly with the opinions and convictions of the better class of Coatesville citizens...

As far as can be learned public sentiment has not in the least been affected by condemning the editorials that have been printed in magazines, and it seems that the people of Chester County alone of all the rest of the country have been the first to regain their composure after the terrible affair and view it in a calm and dispassionate way. The judgement of the Grand Jury in its presentments to the court following the investigation will no doubt reflect the convictions of the great majority of the better class of Coatesville citizens.

The impression left on readers was that the "better class of citizens" in the borough believed the community would best be served if people simply got on with their lives. The newspaper concluded that the jurors "do not seem interested in this matter [Walker's death]," especially after learning of "conditions existing in Coatesville just previous and at the time of the lynching"—a remark the editors apparently did not feel the need to explain.

On Monday, September 4 (Labor Day), the grand jury resumed its inquiry and over the next four days heard from several dozen witnesses drawn from a list of over two hundred names. Members of the borough council were subpoenaed to appear, as were officers of the Coatesville police force and the nurses and orderlies who were on duty at the hospital on the night of the lynching. Also called was Miss Bessie Eaby, the telephone operator who had tried to reach the authorities during the crisis. Vincent Rice, the eighteen-year-old son of the deceased policeman, appeared to answer questions, as did S.G. Kline, president of the Brandywine Fire Company. Burgess Shallcross, Chief Umsted and Officer Howe were each questioned for several hours, with Umsted and Rice each being called back a second time. Apparently, no effort was made to question the several black migrants in Bernardtown who professed to know of Walker prior to his arrival in Coatesville, nor was anyone who claimed to have seen the fateful Rice-Walker confrontation interrogated.

On Saturday, September 9, as ceremonies were beginning in nearby Christiana to commemorate the sixtieth anniversary of the Christiana Riot, the grand jury issued its report to Judge Butler in West Chester and, having completed its charge, asked to be released. The report the jury issued was vague and inconclusive on key points and failed to go beyond the original eight indictments. Although it mildly criticized the Coatesville police force for not reacting promptly to the crisis on Sunday evening, it recommended that no additional arrests be made. In essence, these seventeen men from

Chester County concluded that what could be done had been done and that it would serve no purpose to further investigate the incident. Judge Butler acknowledged the jurors' difficult position and thanked them for their efforts, but he refused to accept their conclusions or their report. Justice would not be served, he argued, if the investigation were simply dropped at this juncture. He therefore ordered the grand jury to continue its investigation until a more thorough and conclusive judgment was rendered. The magistrate's decision prompted several members of the jury to ask for their release from the panel because of pressing business on their farms. Butler agreed to allow them a brief recess to catch up on their affairs, provided they returned to continue the probe. Despite their own misgivings, all of the men agreed to do so.

On Wednesday, September 13, one month after the lynching, the grand jury resumed its inquiry and for seven days listened to over one hundred additional witnesses, many of whom would not agree to testify without being subpoenaed. Prodded by attorneys for the county and the state, and supplied with information from the detectives, the jurors probed deeper than before. In this second round of interviews, they turned their attention to local politicians and businessmen. Representatives of the two major steel mills in Coatesville appeared before the panel, as did numerous Main Street shopkeepers and the local justice of the peace. Among those questioned closely and at length was *Record* editor William Long, especially concerning reports that he instructed a reporter not to go to the site of the lynching lest he be able to identify participants. Long admitted giving his man those instructions, but not for the reason that had been suggested. As word got out that the grand jury would present Judge Butler with another report on Wednesday, September 20, rumors circulated that new arrests were imminent. "SENSATIONAL ARREST EXPECTED IN LYNCHING CASE BEFORE NIGHT," a headline declared in Tuesday's *Record*. According to the newspaper, there was an "air of suppressed excitement around [the] courthouse," and county and state officials were anxious to see the nearly completed grand jury presentment.

At 10:50 a.m. on September 20, the grand jury issued a final report that was shocking in its implications and damning in its judgments. It is hard to say why this second report was so much more conclusive than the first, but with its release the fiction could no longer be maintained that residents of Coatesville played no part in the events of August 13, 1911. Based on information contained in the report, four additional men from Coatesville were arrested. Richard Tucker and Walter Markward were charged with murder. The more sensational warrants, however, were directed at Charles E. Umsted, who had been chief of police for longer than most people could remember, and Officer Stanley Howe, like Umsted a longtime resident of the borough. Both men were charged with involuntary manslaughter for their actions on the evening of August 13. Ironically, Howe had announced only ten days earlier that he would challenge Umsted for the constabulary in the October Republican primary. (It was widely believed that, had he lived, Edgar Rice would have been the one to challenge Umsted.) The grand jury report also censured Jesse Shallcross for his failure to act when presented with irrefutable evidence of what was occurring at the hospital. As chief executive of the borough, the jurors declared, Shallcross should have taken steps to mitigate the worsening situation that Sunday evening.

This second report was remarkable for its candor and detail, and for its general indictment of the citizens of Coatesville. In addition to chiding residents for their "remarkable lack of frankness" during testimony, the jurors noted: "Throughout the whole course of our inquiry, we have been hampered and obstructed by the attitude of the citizens of Coatesville and vicinity, having knowledge of the commissioner of the crime and the identity of the criminals." The panel also concluded that, after the crime, "a conspiracy of silence was formed among the citizens of Coatesville"— in essence, a coverup that pervaded the community, creating innumerable obstacles for investigators. In their 1912 final report on the incident, the state police reinforced this point of a conspiracy of silence, singling out an unnamed officer of the Coatesville police force who intimidated local black residents into not speaking with detectives of the state police.

For the first time, the grand jury not only identified those said to have participated in the lynching but also gave a far different, and certainly more complex, account of the events of August 11–13, 1911. The report raised serious questions about the authority of Edgar Rice, a special policeman for the Worth Brothers, to arrest Zachariah Walker on a public road for carrying a "concealed deadly weapon." Rice was not on company property at the time, had not seen Walker commit a crime and did not have a warrant for Walker's arrest, the jurors noted, and he thus may have been acting improperly. Of course, this indirectly lent credence to Walker's assertion that he had shot Rice in self-defense. As to the matter of whether Walker's abduction and lynching were spontaneous actions by unknown persons, the report concluded that for at least two hours before the lynching, rumors had spread throughout the West End that unnamed parties were going to get Walker. Even as he was being removed from the police station, those on hand muttered that the black man should be lynched. And by seven o'clock, when a crowd estimated at between fifty and one hundred (and later five hundred) people had gathered in front of the Brandywine Fire Station on Main Street, it was clear that some in the crowd had already decided to kill Walker. The jurors noted that "one of the members of the fire company [Mordecai Markward, brother of one of the accused]…realizing the purpose of the crowd, warned some of his fellow members to stay out of the crowd." About this time, the report continued, Al Berry and William Gilbert showed up at the station, having come from the hospital where they had surveyed the situation and spoken with Stanley Howe about the prisoner's condition, and allegedly informed the crowd that it would be a "cinch to get the nigger as there was only one, officer on guard."

According to the jury's report, it was clear that by 8:00 p.m., with people flooding into Coatesville from farms and neighboring townships, a weary Chief Umsted had several times ignored pleas that he go to the hospital and halt the mob. He had even refused to accept the advice of Councilman Richard Gibney, who called for additional men to be deputized to keep the peace. All the while the swelling mob was descending on the hospital grounds. The report further stated that when Officer Howe left Walker's room shortly after 8:30 p.m. to speak with a group of men at the main entrance to the hospital, he did, indeed, deny them entry. But the grand jury concluded that somehow the hospital doors were opened, most likely from the inside; that is, there was no sign of forced entry, as had been reported originally. A group of perhaps twenty-five men—only a small number of them wearing masks, contrary to popular belief—then rushed down the corridor toward Walker's room. At that point, according to the report, Richard Tucker (who lived in the same neighborhood as Howe and whose wife was related to Howe by marriage) emerged from the group and told Howe that he had best offer no resistance. After the two conversed, Howe quietly stepped aside and allowed Walker to be taken from the hospital. Contrary to what the *Record* had reported, the jurors found no evidence that Howe, who stood over six feet tall and carried a loaded nine-shot Colt revolver, had tried to discourage the mob. Despite his testimony that he was roughed up by several men before Tucker appeared, and his own admission that he "was so scared [he] did not know what to do," Howe was declared guilty of the "grossest negligence." Not only had Howe failed to do anything to protect Walker, the report stated, but "he in fact aided and abetted the lynchers in the preparation of the murder of his prisoner" and should therefore be indicted for involuntary manslaughter.

The evidence against Richard Tucker and Walter Markward seemed to be especially damaging. Although Tucker denied it, Howe insisted that Tucker had convinced him to step aside, and his testimony was corroborated by a witness who reported hearing this exchange in Walker's room:

Tucker: "Stanley, is there anything I can do for you?"

Howe: "Tuck, what can I do?"

Tucker: "Stanley, there is no use in your getting hurt in this mob."

Howe also reported that it was Tucker who jested, "Look at that son-of-a-bitch roll" as Walker was dragged away. Other testimony presented to the jury indicated that when the crowd outside the hospital had been unsure of what to do, it was Tucker whom they called out for, and it was an unmasked (and therefore easily identifiable) Tucker who led a group of men into Walker's room. While the evidence suggested that he did not play a part in the actual killing—in his own words, he had remained at the hospital for several hours to "pacify" distraught nurses and patients—the report nonetheless concluded that Tucker appeared to be "one of the originators of the plan to lynch Walker," that it had been prearranged that he would be the one to speak to Howe and that for his role in Walker's abduction he should be indicted for murder. As for Markward, a thirty-one-year-old employee at the main Worth Brothers mill who claimed he was working that evening and did not arrive at the scene of the lynching until after Walker was dead, he, too, was singled out by the grand jury as one of the leaders of the mob. Unnamed witnesses testified that he was conspicuous throughout the evening, and it was Markward who later boasted to a group of teenage boys, "By God, boys, we made a clean job of it!" The jurors thus recommended that Markward also be indicted for murder.

The grand jury's report also revealed that Chief Umsted had not only failed to pursue the lynchers but did not go to the scene of the lynching that night. Furthermore, he had contradicted himself by claiming at different times that he did not really know what was going on, that Dr. Carmichael did not believe Walker was actually being lynched or that by the time he arrived at the hospital the mob was too far ahead of him. The jurors concluded that the constable had failed in his duties, had failed to direct his subordinates properly in a time of crisis and, by bragging openly of Walker's confession in front of the fire station, had actually "aided and abetted" the would-be lynchers, thereby becoming an "accessory to the murder of Zach Walker." On the basis of such misconduct, Umsted was, like Howe, indicted for involuntary manslaughter. In both cases, the jury recommended the lesser offense because it thought the chances of conviction were better. As for the rest of the police force, with the possible exception of Stanley Howe, the report stated, no one made the slightest effort to prevent the lynching, despite the rumors that had circulated throughout the borough for several hours.

For all that its report revealed about the death of Zachariah Walker, the grand jury could only speculate about where the idea had originated. Evidence seemed to suggest that it came from unidentified members of the Brandywine Fire Company, though the jurors were quick to point out that the company itself should not be held responsible. (Ironically, the report noted, after Walker was killed the Brandies passed a resolution condemning the lynching.) Once again, it was the "conspiracy of silence" that led to the jurors' inability to identify members of the company (besides those already mentioned) who were directly involved in the crime. And despite having heard from 161 witnesses, they also failed to identify those who actually set the fire and held Walker over the flames—a crucial omission from an otherwise exhaustive review of the episode. The jurors had no doubt, despite suggestions to the contrary, that Walker's murder was the result of a premeditated, well-crafted conspiracy executed by men and boys with long-standing ties to Coatesville, or that since the commission of the crime the conspiracy had broadened to include a large segment of the community who now remained mute on the critical question of who spearheaded the lynching. A conservative estimate placed 4,000 persons at the scene of Walker's death, but not one voice had been raised in protest during the lynching and not one person had come forward to identify anyone responsible for the act. The existing evidence as to who set the fire was largely circumstantial, a point that would prove critical in the upcoming trials.

Reaction to the grand jury presentment was swift and hostile. The *Record* took the lead, declaring on Friday, September 22, that "word on the street" was that the report was nothing more than a continuation in a long-standing civic feud between West Chester and Coatesville. Rather than coming to grips with the information contained in the report, the newspaper

The Speakman's Hotel, where Coatesville residents gathered to learn news of the court proceedings in West Chester. *Courtesy of the Chester County Historical Society.*

maintained that behind the masquerade of legal formality West Chester was using the incident to give Coatesville a "black eye." In other words, people ought not to mistake what was actually going on in this entire episode. It was also announced that a defense fund had already been started and that a large sum of money would be raised to aid the accused in their trials, which were due to begin in two weeks. A scathing editorial by William Long, the editor of the paper, condemned the manner in which Coatesville had been unfairly put on trial. He implied that the investigation and jury pronouncement were politically motivated, nothing more than a cheap ruse at the borough's expense. And in defense of his community, he claimed it was a well-known fact that West Chester men keep their "dusky belles" behind closed doors and out of sight—an apparent reference to the biblical injunction that he who is without sin should cast the first stone.

After the grand jury report was delivered to the district attorney, Robert Gawthrop said that it was "merely a suggestion of what is to follow." Less than a week later, on Thursday, September 28, four more persons were arrested; three of them subsequently were charged with murder. John Conrad, Louis

Keyser and Ernest White were all from Coatesville and worked at the Lukens mill; nineteen-year-old Lewis Denithorne was a member of the Brandywine Fire Company. Conrad, age seventeen, was the youngest of the four; Keyser and White were both in their mid-twenties. White was released from custody after being interrogated by county officials, but by the time a grand jury considered the culpability of Conrad, Keyser and Denithorne, the first set of trials had already concluded.

Saturday, September 30, was primary election day in Chester County. Nominations for county and municipal offices were at stake, including those of district attorney and chief of police in Coatesville. Before the voting began, Coatesville attorney Walter E. Greenwood accurately predicted to the West Chester newspaper, "Here in Coatesville we will go along as usual and Umsted will be elected Constable just as though nothing had happened." In the contest for the Republican nomination for district attorney, Harris Sproat had the backing of incumbent Robert Gawthrop, who chose not to seek reelection. Sproat was the current assistant district attorney and was expected to take an active role for the prosecution in the upcoming trials. He carried the county by 900 votes but failed to win in Coatesville. In the Republican primary for constable of the borough of Coatesville, Charles Umsted swept eight of the nine precincts in a landslide victory over challengers Albert Jackson, chief of the Lukens force, and Stanley Howe. The incumbent received 765 of 939 votes cast; Howe mustered only 41.

Although it is not surprising that the slated candidates won their contests in the overwhelmingly Republican county, the primary results in Coatesville revealed a great deal about local sentiments on the lynching and the impending prosecutions. On October 2, "UMSTED SWEEPS THE BOROUGH OF COATESVILLE" appeared in boldface across the front page of the *Record*. In an accompanying editorial, Long offered his thoughts on the results of the primary: "In Coatesville, the nomination of Charles E. Umsted by an overwhelming vote goes more than anything to show the feelings of the people of the Town as to the unjustness of the charge which is hanging over him. The voice of the townspeople at the polls must be heard in every section of the county." That same day, the first set of trials for the men accused of the lynching murder of Zachariah Walker began in the county courthouse in West Chester.

Chapter 3
"A DISGRACEFUL TRAVESTY OF JUSTICE"

The Chester County Court of Oyer and Terminer convened in West Chester on October 2, 1911, a day that began with sullen clouds, the lingering remnants of an all-night rain, draped over eastern Pennsylvania. As if on cue, the sky quickly cleared and a beautiful sunny, cool autumn day developed. The weather symbolized the attitude of the citizens of Coatesville in the coming weeks, as gloom and despair gave way to optimism and glee. Within the borough, a natural curiosity was mixed with apprehension. Some residents rode the trolley to West Chester each day to witness the legal proceedings firsthand, while others gathered near the office of the *Coatesville Record* to read the latest news as it was posted on a bulletin board. The trepidation of local inhabitants paralleled a reluctance among the citizens of the county to confront the circumstances of the lynching. Despite the political rivalry between Coatesville and West Chester, residents of both communities shared a sympathy for the accused.

The streets of West Chester and the corridors of the courthouse were unusually crowded that Monday as hundreds of out-of-towners and curious residents came to see the trials. Many hoped to get a seat in the courtroom or perhaps catch a glimpse of the defendants, while others waited patiently outside to hear the latest news. The *West Chester Daily Local News* indicated the significance of the lynching trials by placing photographs of Judge Joseph Hemphill, Judge William Butler Jr., District Attorney Robert S. Gawthrop and County Detective Robert O. Jeffries across the top of page one with the

Chester County Courthouse, West Chester, circa 1911. *Courtesy of the Chester County Historical Society.*

headline "MURDER CASES NOW UNDERWAY." These four men would figure prominently in the trials, as they sought to resolve any doubt about who started the fire that burned Zachariah Walker to death. One other man who would play a significant role was Jesse B. Cunningham, deputy attorney general of Pennsylvania, who represented the state government and acted as prosecuting attorney. Governor John K. Tener had appointed Cunningham, the former Westmoreland County prosecutor, to the post because of his expertise in complicated criminal litigation and because the governor had complete faith in Cunningham's ability to obtain convictions in this shameful episode. Cunningham was considered a solid addition to the prosecution team because of his legal skills, his thoroughness and his steadfastness under pressure—all of which would be taxed by the Coatesville lynching trials. Faced with the difficult task of obtaining convictions or disgracing the judicial system of Pennsylvania, his presence during the trials helped agitate a latent public contempt for state interference in what many residents of Chester County, including Coatesville, perceived to be a local matter.

"A Disgraceful Travesty of Justice"

The prosecution planned to argue in each case that commonwealth law held the people who planned, encouraged or participated in the lynching to be as responsible for Walker's death as those who actually started the fire. This meant that the commonwealth did not have to determine conclusively the person or persons who had struck the match but had only to establish who took an active role in any phase of the lynching. The legal principle of "equal responsibility" was imperative to the prosecution's case and helps explain the commonwealth's assured, almost overconfident public statements that, despite the weight of only circumstantial evidence against the accused, convictions would be obtained. Defense lawyers did not accept the argument of "equal responsibility"; rather, they planned to seek acquittals by establishing reasonable doubt in the minds of the jurors. They were confident it would work to their clients' advantage that the abundance of evidence *was* circumstantial—which had been sufficient, according to the grand jury, to warrant a trial for the accused but which did not point conclusively to the person or persons who had spearheaded the lynching. Members of the jury would find it difficult to accept the principle of "equal responsibility" in what was sure to be an emotionally charged trial, the attorneys reasoned, especially when a guilty verdict could result in the death sentence for so many men and boys. If the jurors had a single reservation, if they were at all uncertain about the guilt of the accused, then they were bound by law to acquit them.

The trials began rather unceremoniously in courtroom number one when Chester Bostic was brought before Judge Hemphill on charges of first-degree murder. Then, in a move that caught courtroom spectators by surprise, the district attorney requested that Bostic be acquitted of all charges. Gawthrop chose not to prosecute the teenager because of the lack of evidence against him and because Bostic had agreed to turn state's evidence in the remaining trials. The young man was "merely a spectator," Gawthrop told the court, and had not taken part in the lynching, yet he "saw fully what occurred," making him a credible witness for the prosecution. The judge directed a verdict of "not guilty," and Bostic was set free. After he left the courtroom, a throng of friends and well-wishers immediately surrounded him. For the first time in nearly seven weeks, he was out of the county jail, and tears of joy flowed down his cheeks. Bostic smugly told friends on the street corner, "I have learned one big lesson from this…I must be careful hereafter about the company I keep and stay away from crowds." He was soon escorted to a

Judge Joseph Hemphill, circa 1885. Hemphill presided over several of the earliest trials before he excused himself. *Courtesy of the Chester County Historical Society.*

nearby hotel, where he stayed at the county's expense for the remainder of the October trials.

Immediately following Bostic's acquittal, proceedings for the second trial began. Nineteen-year-old Joseph Swartz, who allegedly had entered the hospital, removed Walker and helped drag the black man to the burning site, where he then added straw to the funeral pyre, was charged with first-degree murder. Since this was probably the most important of all the lynching trials, three of the most prominent and respected attorneys in Chester County made up Swartz's defense team. Wilmer W. MacElree, known to all as "W.W.," was the legal sage of Chester County and would actually defend Swartz. George S. Dewees and Walter E. Greenwood, who was from Coatesville and was the district attorney's closest friend, would provide additional counsel when needed.

The jury selection in *Commonwealth v. Joseph Swartz* was laborious, as both sides used an unusually large number of challenges. During the initial selection process, which lasted until late in the afternoon, lawyers questioned the entire pool of sixty-two jury candidates and found only eight men acceptable. In an unusual move to secure four additional jurors, Judge Hemphill ordered the courtroom doors closed and directed Sheriff D.M. Golder "to secure talesmen from the spectators in the Court Room." Five people from the crowded room were interviewed, and four were chosen, thus completing the twelve-man jury. Because the pool of jurors had been exhausted, the court called sixty additional candidates for the subsequent trials, thereby contributing to the mounting costs of the prosecution and fueling resentment among county taxpayers. The *West Chester Daily Local News*, which was sympathetic to the prosecution, complained that over $300 a day was being spent on jury costs alone.

Several patterns emerged in the Swartz jury selection process that were repeated in each of the subsequent trials. At least half of the jurors were farmers, and the remainder were either craftsmen or businessmen. With one exception, all of the juries were devoid of mill laborers and unskilled workers. As might be expected, the defense and the commonwealth expressed concern over preconceived notions of guilt or innocence, and both sides rejected potential jurors who had formed an opinion based on local newspaper accounts. Lawyers were especially interested in whether jury candidates held a position on capital punishment, which until 1913 in Pennsylvania meant death by hanging. Prosecuting attorneys rejected anyone who opposed the death penalty, while defense lawyers struck candidates who had "no conscientious scruples against capital punishment." The commonwealth took the additional step of striking "for reason of residence" anyone from Coatesville or neighboring East Fallowfield, Valley or Caln townships. What resulted were juries composed solely of native white residents of Chester County.

Following jury selection and a recess, the Swartz trial moved into courtroom number two, with Judge William S. Butler Jr. presiding. It was late afternoon when the jurors took their seats to hear the opening arguments. The room was filled to capacity with curious spectators, and court officers were forced to lock the doors and grant admission only to those people who had cards signed by District Attorney Gawthrop. One such person was Dr. William Sinclair of Philadelphia, a physician, educator and member of the national board of the National Association for the Advancement of Colored People, who had been sent to monitor the trials. Although he never identified himself to local authorities and his presence was not mentioned in the local newspapers, he filed periodic reports on the proceedings with the NAACP's national office in New York. Born a slave in South Carolina in 1858, Sinclair had long been involved in black advancement activities, both as an early supporter of Booker T. Washington and later as a member of the Committee of Forty, which established the NAACP in 1910. Mary White Ovington remembered him telling the story that his father, a member of the state legislature during Reconstruction, had himself been the victim of a lynch mob.

Deputy Attorney General Cunningham opened the trial by presenting the commonwealth's case against Joseph Swartz. He emphasized the principle of "equal responsibility" and, after outlining the events of August 12–13, carefully noted Swartz's alleged role in the lynching. He also advised the twelve men of the jury: "We are sworn to do our duty to justice without feeling of passion. It is just cases similar to this one which determines how strong the law of our land is." After concluding his hour-long address, Cunningham called the state's first witness. Nathan Rambo, the county surveyor, displayed maps, drawings and pictures of Coatesville and explained to the jury the location of several buildings and the route the mob took that night so the jury would be familiar with the scene of the crime. Following Rambo's testimony, Judge Butler adjourned the court for the day.

The commonwealth's case against Swartz centered in part on eyewitness testimony that linked him to the lynching. As the trial resumed and additional witnesses were called to testify, it became apparent that, while they could remember extensive details of the events of "that quiet Sabbath evening," none of them could positively identify the participants. The first of these witnesses was Mordecai Markward, who described the crowd that had gathered outside the Brandywine Fire Company. Markward testified that he followed the mob to the hospital and later witnessed the burning of Zachariah Walker because "curiosity" took him there. Somewhat reluctantly, and only after intense questioning, did he identify several men, none of whom was accused of participating in the lynching. Not once in his testimony did he mention Swartz. Other witnesses, including Lena Townsend, the hospital superintendent, and Police Officer Stanley Howe, both of whom had been in the hospital at the time the mob stormed inside, also failed to identify Swartz. Even Chester Bostic was of little help to the state, as he did not positively identify Swartz or link him to the crime. The star witness, it turned out, was twenty-year-old Norman Price, one of the accused lynchers. Price testified that Swartz had not only stormed inside the hospital and entered Walker's room with a handkerchief covering his

"A Disgraceful Travesty of Justice"

District Attorney and later Special Prosecutor Robert Gawthrop, who pursued criminal prosecutions in the face of stubborn local opposition. *Courtesy of the Chester County Historical Society.*

face but had helped drag Walker to the burning site and brought straw to add to the fire. The *West Chester Daily Local News*, recognizing how damaging this testimony was to Swartz's defense and seeing an apparent break in the "conspiracy of silence," featured Price's comments and picture on the front page of that afternoon's paper. The *Coatesville Record* boldly proclaimed its own assessment of the case against Swartz: "NOTHING BROUGHT OUT TO CONNECT SWARTZ WITH THE LYNCHING."

Another important aspect of the commonwealth's case against Swartz was his confession to local authorities in the days following the lynching. Robert Gawthrop, Harris Sproat and others had interrogated numerous residents, including Swartz; also present during the interrogations were Captain C.M. Wilhelm of the state constabulary, Coatesville burgess Jesse Shallcross, Chester County detective Jeffries and Police Chief Charles Umsted. At first, Swartz persistently denied "taking part in the lynching," but when the authorities pressed him—"You know you were there"; "You know you are lying"—he broke down and confessed to being in the hospital. Supposedly, Gawthrop then placed his hand on Swartz's shoulder, having already shaken his finger in the young man's face, and instructed Swartz to tell the truth. Finally, according to Shallcross, with everyone in the room "firing" questions, Swartz "admitted, when pressed, that he did assist in carrying the negro and got straw" to set him on fire. When the confession was introduced at the trial, the defense counsel immediately argued that Swartz's will had been "actually subjugated or overcome" and that his "was not a voluntary confession." MacElree labeled the confession "legally improper," declaring that it had been "extorted" in a threatening manner and therefore should not be admitted as evidence. He further accused the authorities of using "coercion and intimidation" to make a nineteen-year-old boy confess to a crime he did not commit.

Both the prosecution and the defense recognized that the outcome of the trial might very well hinge on the admissibility of Swartz's confession into evidence, and neither side was willing to concede its position. Judge Butler, realizing that the proceedings had reached an impasse, dismissed the jury from the courtroom and for nearly an hour heard arguments from Gawthrop and MacElree. Then, after some deliberation, he ruled that Swartz's confession was in fact admissible, based on his interpretation of the rules of evidence. The jury was then reseated, and the commonwealth called the authorities present at Swartz's interrogation to the witness stand. Umsted and Shallcross both testified that the inquiry was exacting and had a threatening tone—Umsted labeled it "a pretty severe grilling"—while Wilhelm and Jeffries stated that the interrogation was conducted fairly and that Swartz was not coerced into admitting his participation in the lynching. Although Wilhelm could not remember specific details of the interrogation, he testified that there was no excessive duress or "sweating," as Shallcross had suggested. The *Record* took delight in Wilhelm's failure to remember certain details, asserting that he had developed "a bad memory similar to that charged up against the Coatesville people with respect to remembering who they saw at the scene of the burning."

In cross-examining these witnesses, the defense counsel continued its attack against the two central points of the commonwealth's case: namely, Swartz's confession and Norman Price's identification of Swartz as an active participant in the lynching. MacElree began with a commentary about the interrogation, but from his client's perspective. He emphasized that Swartz was a mere boy who had been easily cajoled by the older men, themselves imposing legal authorities, and that his confession had been extracted under duress, the "so called 'third degree' method." To bolster his client's position and cast further doubt, specifically on Price's testimony, MacElree called several witnesses who testified that Swartz did not participate in the lynching

"A Disgraceful Travesty of Justice"

Wilmer W. MacElree, the fiery
Chester County defense attorney.
Taken from his *Side Lights of the
Bench and Bar in Chester County.*
*Courtesy of the Chester County
Historical Society.*

at all. They claimed that he had observed the events from a safe distance and then returned to Coatesville, where he met some girls. Not only did their testimony provide Swartz with an alibi, but it also helped establish some uncertainty in the jurors' minds as to the validity of his confession and of Price's statements while under oath. Supplementing MacElree's eloquent defense were Swartz's actions in the courtroom. The defendant, who never took the witness stand to testify on his own behalf, appeared nervous throughout the trial and spent much of his time sobbing almost uncontrollably. Such childlike behavior did not escape the jury's attention.

This first trial ended in the early evening of the second day. The jury received its charge from Judge Butler, in which he emphasized the principle of "equal responsibility," and began its deliberations at 8:15 p.m. Joseph Swartz was returned to jail under the assumption that the jury had abundant evidence to consider—specifically, the conflicting eyewitness accounts and the contrasting presentations of his confession—and could not possibly render a verdict until the next day. However, less than two hours later, the jury reached a decision that had required only two votes. Rather than wait until morning, Butler called prosecution and defense lawyers to the courthouse to hear the verdict. Despite the late hour (it was after 10:30 p.m.), a sizable crowd gathered in the courtroom. Swartz was brought in from his jail cell and "several times broke down and cried" while waiting for the jury's decision. "Not guilty came from the lips of the jury as one," observed the *Daily Local News*, "and Swartz, who had been leaning forward listening to every word, gave a long sigh and then buried his head in his hands and cried while...[MacElree] turned to the jury and thanked them for their prompt and just verdict." Gawthrop and Cunningham were stunned to have lost a case that was, according to them, legally indisputable. A group of well-wishers quickly descended upon Swartz and escorted the elated young man outside the courthouse, where an even larger crowd cheered his acquittal. Swartz told those who gathered around him, "I have been in jail for 47 days and they will always be remembered as the most terrible in my life." All he wanted to do now was to return to work and a normal life. Chester Bostic, acquitted earlier in the week, offered his congratulations, and the two "laughed happily" about the verdict, hoping similar decisions would be rendered for the others. Swartz then went to MacElree's home as his guest for the night.

Several hundred Coatesville residents were eagerly waiting outside the *Record* office on Main Street for news of the verdict. The newspaper had made special arrangements for the verdict to be telephoned to its office immediately after it was announced. It was nearly eleven o'clock when Owen Spackman rushed onto Main Street and shouted, "Not guilty!" His words brought a cheer from the crowd, and within minutes the news spread throughout the town. People flocked into the streets to join in the celebration, and when one of Swartz's attorneys, Walter E. Greenwood, arrived, the mob pressed around him to offer congratulations. Some even declared of Greenwood, "Let's put him up for District Attorney right away." They felt jubilant as well as vindicated; the first of their own had stood trial and been acquitted. As for the person who had betrayed the "conspiracy of silence," the *West Chester Daily Local News* noted: "Coatesville people will not get the band out to give a reception for Norman Price, who...told what others had done."

The next morning, an obviously frustrated deputy attorney general publicly denounced the verdict as "a disgraceful travesty of justice." For only the second time in his legal career, Jesse Cunningham openly criticized a jury's decision, lamenting, "I can't understand how...[a jury] can render a verdict of not guilty in cases where it was absolutely shown that the defendant was a participant in the crime for which he is being tried. Even when the defendant had admitted that he gave physical aid, he is acquitted, and his confession is discounted." Despite the evidence, the prosecutor asserted, "a Chester County jury…by its verdict, placed itself squarely on record as favoring mob government, mob murder, and mob justice." He added that such action was tantamount to declaring "that lynch law has supplanted the law of the land." Betrayed by his own emotions, Cunningham went on to criticize Swartz for exercising his Fifth Amendment right against self-incrimination. The deputy attorney general said he found it distasteful that the accused had not taken the witness stand to declare his guilt or innocence under oath. Such railing on Cunningham's part was, of course, both improper and careless and did not help the state's cause in West Chester. In fact, his behavior did much to undermine the credibility of the commonwealth's position. MacElree called the outburst "unprofessional and without foundation" and then added, "I know of no provision of the criminal law that makes the opinion of a deputy Attorney General equivalent to proof in any court of justice." An extremely frustrated Cunningham told a friend that "it was more difficult to get at the truth here than it was in the Capitol graft cases." The commonwealth's disappointment and frustration would grow with each passing day in the remaining trials.

On the morning of Cunningham's public outburst, George Stoll was brought to trial before Judge Hemphill. The now sixteen-year-old stood accused of helping to remove Walker from the hospital and participating in the burning. Jury selection took the entire morning. Two young, inexperienced attorneys, Howard Troutman and J. Paul MacElree (the son of W.W. MacElree), represented Stoll. Troutman had passed the Pennsylvania bar examination on Monday, and now, on Thursday, was making his first court appearance, in a murder trial, no less! The newspapers referred to Troutman and MacElree as "green" lawyers, but their selection was a ploy to emphasize the youth of their client. To ensure that no serious errors were made by the attorneys for the defense, several experienced lawyers from firms in West Chester sat in the public area of the courtroom and provided counsel to Troutman and MacElree when necessary.

Jesse Cunningham opened the Stoll trial with a review of the lynching and a declaration, obviously with reference to his earlier public comments, that this case pitted "law and order and government against mob law, disorder and anarchy." As in the Swartz trial, he then explained to the jury the various degrees of murder and the legal principle of "equal responsibility." Following this, the prosecutor called several of Stoll's friends to the stand, all of whom had to be subpoenaed before they would appear in court. These witnesses, particularly Charles Whitely and Raymond Day, recalled the events of the lynching with remarkable clarity, but they did not identify any of the mob leaders; at best, they were evasive about whom they had seen and what they had heard that night. After lengthy questioning, however, each of Stoll's friends testified that Stoll had been on the hospital porch and had told Officer Howe to "open the door, for [the mob] would get Walker anyway." Howe corroborated this testimony when he took the witness stand, adding that Stoll had also come inside the hospital. Other witnesses placed Stoll in the crowd near the fire, but they maintained that he was an observer, not a participant. Once again, Norman Price proved to be the commonwealth's star witness. Although he failed to identify the person(s) who had struck the match, he did testify that he and Stoll had gone up to the hospital porch together and had tried to convince Howe to open the door. He also admitted that they had entered the hospital and had helped drag Walker outside and down the country lane to the burning site.

Near the end of Price's testimony, which was considered damaging to the defense, an event took place that indicated the growing frustration of prosecutors Gawthrop and Cunningham. After a long, disruptive afternoon of questioning witnesses, the district attorney abruptly beseeched Judge Hemphill to protect "the Commonwealth's officials" from "remarks of an insulting nature." Gawthrop was referring to a group of elderly lawyers seated in the back of the courtroom who had been essentially heckling the prosecution throughout the afternoon. Their chief insult was to claim that Cunningham was doing more for the defense than for the prosecution. Hemphill thought he could avoid a controversy by adjourning court for the day, but as he left the courtroom, several attorneys rushed toward Gawthrop, and harsh words were exchanged. Someone called the district attorney a "fool" and claimed his conduct was "a grand stand play" that demonstrated "ill breeding." His face flush with anger and his fists clenched, Gawthrop seemed ready for a fight. However, he quickly recovered his composure and refused to join the fray, leaving the courtroom without further comment. Later that evening, Cunningham again publicly expressed his frustration and complete dismay with the course of events, his comments reflecting the growing state-local tensions. He admitted that the commonwealth was having "difficulty" with the prosecution and that his presence in West Chester had complicated matters, but he genuinely believed that there was enough evidence to obtain a number of convictions. Still, he hinted that all of the cases might end the way Swartz's did, since that case had been "the strongest of them all." The *Daily Local News* agreed, observing the next day that "street talk lionizes Swartz and makes martyrs of the men in jail" while "officers of the law are jeered." Public sentiment, the newspaper reported, was that "no one shall be punished for the Coatesville lynching."

On Friday afternoon, October 6, George Stoll's trial ended. The highlight of the concluding hours came when Stoll took the witness stand and testified that he had not participated in the lynching. In the closing arguments for the defense, Howard Troutman frequently emphasized his client's "extreme youth," expressing doubt that a boy could take part in a lynching, let alone lead a mob of adults. J. Paul MacElree struck a responsive chord among those gathered in the courtroom when he stated, "The Deputy Attorney General has referred to the tainted air of East Fallowfield Township, but it is no more polluted than the atmosphere of Harrisburg." Then he added, just in case his point had been missed, "I want to say to the Deputy Attorney General that Chester County does not have to be admonished of its duties by the State." The inexperienced lawyer went right to the heart of the matter when he declared that, contrary to the prosecution's claim, "this was not a trial of mob law but a case of a boy on trial for his life." Then he reminded the jury that to find young George Stoll guilty of murdering Zachariah Walker might mean the boy's execution. Unable to locate anyone who would identify the person(s) responsible for lighting the fire, the prosecution could only repeat that several eyewitnesses had seen Stoll actively participate in the lynching and he was therefore guilty as charged.

Following Judge Hemphill's instructions, the jury deliberated for less than one hour before returning with a verdict of "not guilty." A jubilant Stoll ran from the courtroom and, once outside, was hoisted onto his friends' shoulders and carried through the streets of West Chester, trailed by a group of forty boys, all cheering and yelling. Several hundred people again had gathered along Main Street in Coatesville to await news of the verdict, and the *Record* office was besieged with telephone calls about the trial. Within twenty minutes of Stoll's acquittal, the newspaper had published a special edition to announce the verdict, and the entire edition of several thousand copies was promptly sold out. The commonwealth had lost two major cases in less than a week, the last one to inexperienced attorneys. It appeared increasingly likely that the public was correct in its belief that no one would be punished for the lynching.

After reconsidering its strategy over the weekend, on Monday morning the prosecution brought the first adult to trial. Thirty-seven-year-old Joseph Schofield, a master mechanic for the Conestoga Traction Company (a trolley car company in Chester County) and a specially deputized police officer with the authority to arrest any drunk and disorderly people who rode the weekend trolleys, was accused of murder, stemming from his alleged participation in the lynching. Schofield was represented by Thomas "Tommy" Lack of Coatesville. Jury selection consumed most of the morning session, as fifty-seven men were interviewed before the necessary twelve were selected. Prosecutors prudently rejected those men who were jurors in the two previous trials as well as anyone from Coatesville and its neighboring townships.

The commonwealth's case against Schofield focused on two points: that he had led the group of men on the hospital porch; and that he had

A view of the trolley and horse-drawn wagon on Main Street, Coatesville, circa 1905. *Courtesy of the Chester County Historical Society.*

brought wood to add to the fire. Jesse Cunningham not only opened the trial but conducted virtually the entire prosecution, making this his trial in many people's eyes. Robert Gawthrop sat in silence throughout most of the proceedings, asking only a few questions during cross-examinations and providing virtually no assistance to Cunningham until the end was in sight. To courtroom observers, it appeared that discord had developed between the prosecutors and that the district attorney was distancing himself from the deputy attorney general because of the growing public sentiment against the intrusion of the state government into local affairs. The prosecution's two principal witnesses were Stanley Howe and Norman Price. Howe testified that he had known Schofield for four years and could positively identify him as one of the men on the hospital porch but that Schofield had never entered the building. Price swore under oath that, as he sat on a fence railing at the lynching site, a man brushed past him shouting, "Look out, let me through with this load of wood." Although it was nighttime and the man wore dark clothes and a dark hat, Price was absolutely positive that the man was Joseph Schofield (whom he had known for one year, though he had never talked to him). Cunningham called this testimony the "strongest and only evidence" against the defendant.

Following the precedent established in the earlier trials, Lack defended his client with relative ease by successfully discounting Price's testimony. He pointed out that no other witness could corroborate Price's identification of Schofield as the man who had carried wood to the fire—an identification Price made even though he had never met Schofield and had only heard his voice infrequently while riding on the trolley cars. Lack also revealed that Schofield had worn a light-colored gray suit and hat on the night of the lynching, not dark clothes. A parade of witnesses attested to Schofield's attire, and to add credibility to the defense, Schofield wore the same suit when he took the witness stand. Schofield admitted that he had been on the hospital porch, but he said that his intent was to offer Stanley Howe some assistance, not to incite the lynch mob. "I thought I would try to prevent it," he explained, and as a special trolley deputy who frequently helped the police "whenever they called on me," his presence on the porch was not unusual—or so the defense contended. Several witnesses disclosed that Schofield had made no effort to prevent the lynching, either on the hospital porch or at the fire. But he insisted that he "just went with the crowd" down the country road, that he "couldn't do anything to prevent the work of the mob" once they had decided to burn Walker. Courtroom spectators later said that Schofield made a convincing presentation from the witness stand. The *Record* observed that "Price's testimony was worthless" and that "the case fell flat" after Schofield's statements.

At the conclusion of the testimony, Robert Gawthrop surprised the court when he rose to ask Judge Butler if there was substantial evidence for the trial to continue. He conceded that the commonwealth's case against Schofield was based on conflicting testimony but believed that there were "suspicious circumstances" that could not be ignored. Schofield was too close to the events to have just watched, the district attorney reasoned, and therefore must have participated or even assumed a leadership role. Furthermore, there were two eyewitness accounts of his participation, although neither had been substantiated. Butler briefly reviewed the case for the jury, noting, "The only actual aid to this lynching that the evidence tends to show this defendant gave was carrying wood to the fire." Then, despite his earlier statements in support of the prosecution of everyone involved in the horrible crime, he made a startling pronouncement, one that the prosecution could not have anticipated. Turning to the jurors, the judge declared: "The weight of the Commonwealth's testimony tends to but suspicion. I believe that the investigation has been conducted most properly, but I would ask of you that you render a verdict of 'Not Guilty' from your seats." Without leaving the courtroom, the jury complied with Butler's request and declared Schofield "not guilty." Gawthrop and Cunningham offered no protest to this directed verdict, although their frustration was obvious to courtroom observers.

Anticipating an outburst in the courtroom, Butler told the crowd that he would not tolerate "any demonstration" while he was on the bench. The friends of Joseph Schofield thus waited until they were in the streets to begin their celebration. Nearly 1,500 people jammed Main Street in Coatesville to await the arrival of Schofield on the evening trolley. A huge ovation greeted him as he stepped from the car, and he was immediately swept down the street in a wave of congratulations and adulation. Later that evening, Schofield went home to nearby Parkesburg, where he was met by another welcoming crowd. As part of the celebration, Schofield was carried to his house on the shoulders of jubilant well-wishers. Clearly, a pattern had begun to emerge in the trials, acquittals and celebrations for the accused.

On Wednesday morning, October 10, the fourth trial began. Jury selection in the Oscar Lamping case was amazingly brief, taking only forty minutes.

Coatesville's Stephenson House, circa 1911. *Courtesy of the Chester County Historical Society.*

The commonwealth used few of its challenges and even permitted several men who were jurors in the earlier trials, as well as two Parkesburg men, to sit in judgment of Lamping. Close observers believed that the prosecution was "thoroughly disheartened" and that the decision to reseat certain jurors for this trial suggested its seeming surrender of any hope of obtaining convictions. Because the commonwealth had failed thus far to persuade a single jury of the credibility of its position of "equal responsibility," prosecutors decided to pursue a second-degree murder charge against Lamping. This new strategy meant that the state need only demonstrate that Lamping had played a role in the events that led to Walker's death, not that he had planned the lynching or directed the mob.

Jesse Cunningham opened the prosecution by accusing Lamping of instigating the lynching with the statement, "I will lead the crowd if anyone will follow." As in the previous trials, Norman Price's testimony was integral to the commonwealth's case. Price stated that in the hours before the lynching, he and some friends had been discussing the murder of Edgar

Rice with various members of the growing crowd outside the Brandywine Fire Company. At about 8:00 p.m., Price and approximately fifty others were on their way to the hospital when they met William Gilbert and Al Berry, who were returning to town. According to Price, Gilbert and Berry told the group that "it would be a cinch to get the nigger" but that more people were needed to accomplish the task. When the group returned to the Brandywine Fire Company to seek volunteers, Price recounted, Lamping told the assembled throng that "he would lead the crowd." Although the grand jury report substantiated what Price told the court, the commonwealth had no other witness to corroborate his testimony, a point that defense attorney J. Paul MacElree made abundantly clear during the cross-examination. Every other witness testified that they heard someone shout, "I will lead the crowd if anyone will follow" (or something close to that), but no one was able to positively identify that person. It seemed as though the "conspiracy of silence" remained intact.

To further refute the prosecution's case, Lamping waived his right against self-incrimination and took the witness stand. He testified that he had

Main Street looking east from Davy's Drug Store. Note the horse-drawn carriages. *Courtesy of the Frank Pennegar Collection and the Chester County Historical Society.*

listened to Police Chief Umsted's speech to the crowd at the Brandywine Fire Company and then left to spend the evening with his wife and some friends; only after Walker had been taken from the hospital and burned did he learn what had happened. Lamping swore that he had led no lynch mob nor been involved in any way with the lynching itself. Several witnesses, including his wife, verified his testimony. In his closing arguments, MacElree informed the jury, "There is no evidence against Oscar Lamping except that of Norman Price, and he is not to be believed." Lamping "had nothing to do in instigating the mob," his attorney declared, and the only reasonable verdict was acquittal.

The entire trial lasted only several hours, making it the briefest of the lynching trials. In his charge to the jury, Judge Hemphill emphasized that the commonwealth was seeking a conviction on the charge of second-degree murder, meaning the jurors must determine Lamping's complicity rather than his actual participation in the lynching. The jury retired to deliberations at 2:40 p.m. and less than thirty minutes later returned a verdict of "not guilty" before a sparse crowd in courtroom number two. Lamping embraced his wife and "with a merry party of friends" returned triumphantly to Coatesville. "Like the other acquitted men in the lynching cases," the *West Chester Daily Local News* reported, Coatesville gave Lamping a warm welcome home. A large crowd had gathered at the trolley station, and he "received quite an ovation" as he stepped out of the car. Eager friends and well-wishers shook his hand and patted him on the back as they escorted him to his Chestnut Street home.

While the jury in *Commonwealth v. Oscar Lamping* was deliberating, the dual trial of William Gilbert and Albert Berry commenced before Judge Butler. The prosecution decided to try these men together because their cases were closely interrelated, a strategy that the defense attorneys did not challenge. Since neither Gilbert nor Berry had been implicated in the actual lynching, the commonwealth once again pressed for convictions for second-degree murder. The deputy attorney general intended to prove that together Gilbert and Berry had been in Walker's hospital room before the lynching and had returned to the growing crowds in Coatesville to inform people about the situation within the hospital. Cunningham portrayed these men as spies or scouts whose report served to incite the mob. Gilbert had allegedly informed a gang of boys who were walking to the hospital that Officer Howe was the only man on duty and that it would be "a cinch to get the nigger." They also allegedly told the boys that Howe had said "the nigger ought to be hung" but that more people were needed "to get Walker." And Berry had allegedly blurted out that "there ought to be 500 men there if they were going to lynch him." The prosecution, confident that it had a very strong case against the two men, even "declared that if a conviction was not obtained in this case it would be beyond the power of humans to obtain one, and God alone could secure it."

Once again the commonwealth's optimism was based on the testimony of key eyewitnesses Norman Price and Stanley Howe. Price declared that he and a group of boys had met Gilbert and Berry along the "flats" as the men were returning from the hospital and that they had reported on Walker's location in the hospital, the lack of security and the need to round up a number of men to take care of Walker. But his repeated testimony, which was again unsubstantiated, had apparently eroded his credibility as a witness. Calling Price to the witness stand, the *Record* sardonically observed, "was tiresome to not only prosecution, court and jury, but to the spectators, his story having been threshed over so much." The paper declared that Price was "the one last losing hope of the Commonwealth," and others referred to him as the "human adding machine," spewing information that lacked substance and verification. Howe stated that Gilbert and Berry had been in Walker's hospital room at about 7:45 p.m. and that the three men had talked about Walker, his capture and how Berry had earlier prevented Walker's captors from lynching him. When Dr. Carmichael telephoned to say that Walker needed to rest and should be left alone, Howe testified, Gilbert and Berry had left the hospital.

In defending his clients, Tommy Lack turned Howe's testimony to their advantage. During cross-examination, the burly policeman stated that he had never discussed lynching or wanting Walker hanged with Gilbert and Berry, and Lack hoped this flat denial would discredit Price's testimony about statements Howe had made. According to Howe, Gilbert and Berry had come to learn about Walker's physical condition and nothing else; since Berry had helped capture Walker, it was only natural that he would be curious about Walker's self-inflicted wounds. Howe called it a friendly visit, with no other apparent motive. Then Lack put both Berry and Gilbert on the witness stand to defend themselves. Berry discussed at length his role in capturing Walker and how he had prevented several men from lynching him by threatening to shoot anyone who touched the black man. He declared that he had tried to notify the authorities about a lynch mob headed toward the hospital on Sunday night but that the police chief had refused to listen. Berry disavowed recruiting more men for a lynch mob and in fact turned the tables on Price, claiming that Price was the one who had tried to organize a lynch mob and had asked Gilbert and Berry to join in. Gilbert essentially corroborated Berry's recollection of the meeting with Price, declaring that Price had announced, "We're going to lynch that nigger tonight. We're looking for a leader."

At the conclusion of the prosecution's summation, Judge Butler delivered a bold and lengthy charge to the jury. Having presided over most of the cases, he was keenly aware of the evidence, the participants and the juries' obvious reluctance to render convictions. His charge—in effect, a statement about the earlier trials—included an appeal for justice, which the *Record* claimed "seemed to favor a conviction." Touching on the jury's regard for humanity, Butler declared that the slow lynching, condoned by the mob, was a warning "that the veneer of civilization is very thin; that the disposition to return to savagery is strong; that men and boys can with shocking ease be enlisted in a rebellion against the law." Walker's death should not, according to the trial judge, go unpunished. Then, striking at the very heart of the commonwealth's failure to obtain convictions, he proclaimed:

> *It is wholly unimportant to know who played the most prominent part, whose words or acts most contributed to Walker's death. His destruction was the result of the combined words and acts of a number of men and the law holds them all equally responsible for his destruction. The men who originated, suggested, or by words encouraged the lynching, and those who in the end happened to be the ones who actively and actually destroyed Walker are all equally guilty.*

The jurors paid "close attention" to the judge's charge, the newspapers reported, and then left to deliberate. In slightly more than one hour, they handed down two separate verdicts, finding both Gilbert and Berry "not guilty." The hasty deliberation and the acquittals took the commonwealth and numerous spectators "completely by surprise." Butler left the courtroom without a word, but the *Record* indicated that he was "displeased." Unlike the other trials, there was no loud celebration of the decision, despite the large gallery in the courtroom. Perhaps the people had grown accustomed to routine acquittals in the lynching cases.

Judge Butler announced that the trials of William Gilbert and Al Berry would be the last of the court's October session, a decree that had important implications for those awaiting trial. The remaining cases for those men still in jail, as well as for policemen Charles Umsted and Stanley Howe, were placed on the January docket. This meant that Walter Markward, Richard Tucker and Norman Price, who had been denied bail because of the charges against them, were now eligible to post bail. After nearly two months in jail, Markward and Tucker were "liberated" when several prominent businessmen posted a $5,000 bond for each man. Price's father put up a $2,000 bond, and the "star witness for the Commonwealth," as the newspapers called him, went home to the family dairy farm outside Coatesville.

After the October trials concluded, three more people were charged with murder and complicity in the lynching of Zachariah Walker. Lewis Keyser, John Conrad, Lewis Denithorne and Ernest White, who were arrested on September 28, were brought before Justice of the Peace S.M. Paxson on Friday, October 13, for arraignment. Robert Gawthrop and Jesse Cunningham made brief presentations of evidence against the young men, even calling several witnesses. They asked that Keyser, Conrad and Denithorne be charged with murder because each allegedly had helped drag Walker from the hospital. In addition, sixteen-year-old Conrad had apparently struck Walker several times with a fence railing to keep him in the fire. Paxson agreed to the commonwealth's request and charged each of the three with murder. Gawthrop and Cunningham requested that Ernest White be discharged since "there was no evidence against" him, and that request was also granted. Keyser, Conrad and Denithorne were sent back to jail until a grand jury could be called. Because of the seriousness of the charge, the squire refused to set bail, which had the effect of keeping the accused in jail until the final disposition of their cases, which could take months.

The local public remained sympathetic toward both the acquitted and the accused who awaited trial. Perhaps West Chester resident William H. Underwood, who had no connection with the trials except as a curious citizen, expressed this best when he said, "Someone did the lynching, but nobody wants to convict boys who were in the crowd. If I had been there, and a boy again, I would have been on the front row." Judging from the easy acquittals, most residents of Chester County probably shared Underwood's feelings. After the October trials, newspapers in Pennsylvania and throughout the nation no longer placed stories about the lynching trials on their front pages, and even in Coatesville the headlines ceased, if only temporarily. The topic of conversation in Chester County in mid-October 1911 turned to baseball and the World Series matchup between the Philadelphia Athletics and the New York Giants. Most people wanted to forget that the lynching had ever taken place, and some blamed the commonwealth for prolonging the ordeal with so many prosecutions. Robert Gawthrop acknowledged this during the last trial with his remark that "there appears to be a shifting of responsibility, until some scarcely believe there was a lynching affair in Coatesville." "I thought we would be able to convict some of those accused," Cunningham lamented, "but the juries seemed to see things in a different light."

As the November elections approached, neither Gawthrop nor Cunningham was certain of their continued involvement in the cases. Furthermore, a cloud of uncertainty hung over the commonwealth's efforts to prosecute the lynchers of Zachariah Walker.

Chapter 4
"To Humiliate the Administration of Justice"

A lthough the lynching trials and public officials' comments related to that topic adorned newspaper headlines, the pending November elections soon took precedence. At stake were county offices, particularly that of district attorney; in Coatesville, the most prominent positions were three seats on the borough council and the office of constable. The race for district attorney was dignified and did not generate much political excitement, due principally to the respect for and influence of Robert S. Gawthrop. Since Gawthrop's term as district attorney was coming to an end, his assistant, Harris Sproat of West Chester, seemed the likely successor. Sproat, who received the crucial Republican Party endorsement and Gawthrop's support, won the election by a comfortable margin. By contrast, the election for constable spurred what the newspapers called the "usual interest" in politics, and it quickly became a sordid campaign.

Despite his pending trial on the charge of involuntary manslaughter in the lynching of Zachariah Walker, Coatesville police chief Charles E. Umsted sought reelection. His foremost rival was Keystone candidate Frank Davis, an engineer with Worth Brothers who mounted a good campaign against the longtime incumbent. Faced with the possibility of losing, Umsted resorted to ruthless tactics. On the eve of the election, he dismissed John B. Jackson, whom the *Record* called "the big colored police officer," from the force for dereliction of duty; in truth, Jackson was fired because he apparently did not work hard enough to support the chief's campaign. Policemen in Coatesville

Looking down Main Street toward the commercial district, 1911. Note the earthen road and trolley tracks. *Courtesy of the Chester County Historical Society.*

were, in effect, political appointees, and they were expected to gather votes for their superiors while working their beats (a lesson Edgar Rice had learned when he was dismissed from the force in 1910). Although Umsted subsequently lost in the predominantly black eighth and ninth precincts, he carried Coatesville's other seven precincts and won easily. (Coincidentally, Harris Sproat, who participated in the prosecution of the alleged lynchers, also failed to carry the black districts.) The day after his reelection, several of Umsted's close friends, including *Record* editor William W. Long, gave him a magnificent banquet of wild duck with all the trimmings. Diners gathered at the Speakman's Hotel to celebrate the election victory, and Umsted "modestly accepted the congratulations" and a gold pen to honor his good work in the community. The testimonial dinner was characterized by "wit and humor," the *Record* reported in its front-page coverage of the event.

Amid the election excitement and the posttrial publicity, the citizens of Coatesville continued to rationalize the lynching. Numerous residents remarked on how violent the town had become since the influx of foreigners (some called them "aliens") and especially blacks from the South. Although the police were putting up a brave fight and were "busy on two forms of danger"—people carrying concealed weapons and drifters—local police protection was seemingly inadequate. Despite their objections to the commonwealth's involvement in the investigation, people began to call for the establishment of a state police headquarters in Coatesville to help curtail the lawlessness. Led by its editor, the *Record* reinforced the idea that lawlessness and violence were growing. In the weeks following the lynching trials, the newspaper was replete with stories describing alleged violent crimes committed by blacks. Time and again these front-page reports reminded readers that whites were often the victims of these crimes and that the perpetrators were drifters who had no ties to the community; frequently, they appeared simultaneously with news of the latest developments in the lynching investigation or the pending trials. The cumulative effect was to present southern blacks as a criminal element in Coatesville, a perception that seemed to justify the burning of Zachariah Walker.

In a telling front-page article entitled "Zach Walker Caused Town's Martial Law," the *Record* reported on November 20 that Walker had a history of criminal activity before arriving in Coatesville. An unnamed Lebanon, Pennsylvania resident was quoted as saying, "You folks down there [in Coatesville] surely made no mistake in getting hold of a bad negro when you ran down that man Walker." Walker supposedly had worked for the American Iron and Steel Company in 1902, a center of labor violence in eastern Pennsylvania, where he was "held in fear generally" and was arrested several times for "boisterous conduct." When a strike occurred at the mill and the company brought in black strikebreakers, Walker allegedly led "a mob of his own color" in protest. He "took a leading part in the rioting" that broke out near the mills and was arrested after state militia occupied the town and martial law was declared. A local man apparently "informed the authorities that [Walker] was the ring leader of the trouble," and after his release from jail, Walker was literally run out of town. The story concluded with a statement designed to appeal to Coatesville citizens' sentiments: "Zach Walker came here [Lebanon] when we knew little about negroes. Others followed him and the worst trouble we ever had in the mills was due to him and his followers."

News of Walker's alleged criminal activities was a revelation to the citizens of Coatesville and must have reaffirmed their attitude toward the lynching; no one seemed to mind that the story rested upon the distant memory and wild charges of one man who was never identified by name. Although there had been a strike and labor violence over the use of black strikebreakers in Lebanon,

The Hotel Coatesville, circa 1911, outside of which the lynch mob gathered near the Brandywine Fire Station. *Courtesy of the Chester County Historical Society.*

Pennsylvania, in 1902, Walker's name was not mentioned in any accounts of the incident. Furthermore, there was no evidence to indicate that Walker was ever in Lebanon. The *Record* suggested, however, that residents could find solace in lynching Walker. Coatesville was not a "blot on civilization," as some outsiders claimed; rather, its citizens had removed a blot on civilization.

That same week, the National Association for the Advancement of Colored People held a highly publicized antilynching meeting at the Ethical Culture Hall in New York City. The timing was not coincidental. In September and October, *The Crisis* had published extensive commentary on the Coatesville trials, and W.E.B. Du Bois's editorial had offered a stinging rebuke of the community. In October, the board of directors of the NAACP had discussed at length this northern lynching and conceived a national rally to protest not only Walker's death but all lynchings in America. On November 15, 1911, Oswald Garrison Villard, chairman of the board of the NAACP, presided over an evening meeting attended by some four hundred people. Despite lackluster fundraising, the association remained determined to monitor events in Coatesville and to bring Walker's assailants to justice.

Although William Sinclair, the association's observer during the October trials, had reported to the executive committee that he was satisfied "the prosecuting attorney had done his job," other NAACP officials felt the assessment was shortsighted and began their own inquiry. This new effort was a bold step for the fledgling civil rights organization, as it signaled a commitment to direct intervention in a sensitive local matter. Mary Dunlop Maclean, managing editor of *The Crisis*, went to Coatesville in November and conducted a series of interviews; and on at least one occasion, Oswald Garrison Villard also visited the community to meet with sympathetic townspeople. In December, following Maclean's and Villard's reports to the board of directors, the NAACP decided to devote all the monies raised at that Ethical Culture Hall meeting, as well as resources from its legal redress fund, "to an investigation of the Coatesville lynching with a view of obtaining information which would induce the authorities to continue the work of prosecuting those guilty of this inexcusable and inhuman crime." A special Coatesville Committee was established within the association to coordinate the investigation, which was to be independent of the commonwealth's efforts.

On Maclean's recommendation, the William Burns Detective Agency was hired to conduct a clandestine inquiry. During the winter of 1911–12, two Burns agents, who were careful to mask their true intentions (even District Attorney Gawthrop and Deputy Attorney General Cunningham were unaware of their activities), operated a restaurant in Coatesville as a front to gather information. Over a period of two months, they befriended local citizens who might have some knowledge of the Walker lynching; then, as the spring court term approached, they abruptly sold the establishment and left town. For its work, the Burns Agency was paid nearly $2,400, a substantial sum for the often financially strapped NAACP. The detectives' report would be instrumental, however, in the association's efforts to sustain the prosecution when all hope seemed lost.

The commonwealth, having chosen not to relinquish its desire for prosecution after the rebuff of the October trials, resumed its investigation with renewed vigor. State police and detectives in Coatesville persisted in their search for more evidence, and one detective was quoted as saying, "We're going to get the instigators in the Zach Walker burning and don't you forget it." The prosecutors prepared for the pending cases with "unusual care" amid a steady stream of rumors and speculation about the defendants. The *Record* had it "on good authority" that the men already tried would be arrested again on the "lesser charge of rioting." It was also rumored that Gawthrop would remain in charge of the prosecution (even though his term as district attorney expired in January) because he knew the cases better than anyone and because Sproat, the new district attorney, was relatively inexperienced. Given the local reaction to his presence in the courtroom, it was said that Jesse Cunningham probably would not return to continue the prosecution. Earlier, both the Coatesville and West Chester papers had speculated that, because of the commonwealth's failure to obtain convictions in Chester County, the prosecution would apply for a change of venue. As the January court term drew near, they reported that the strongest cases were against Lewis Denithorne and Lewis Keyser, who probably would be tried first, even though neither had been indicted yet. Another rumor circulated that the prosecution might reduce the charges against Denithorne and Keyser from murder to rioting in order to obtain convictions—which prompted several previous jury members to comment that, if that had been the case in October, there would have been a few convictions.

At the end of December 1911, the commonwealth began formal action to continue the lynching cases. Robert Gawthrop was sworn in as special attorney general to try the remaining cases, while Jesse Cunningham was ordered to continue his assistance in the prosecution.

As the leader of the prosecution, Gawthrop announced the commonwealth's plans for the remaining trials. At the beginning of the court term scheduled for January 29, he would ask for a continuance on the grounds that the prosecution required more time to prepare its cases. Given the complicated nature of these cases and the difficulty in gathering evidence, the continuance probably would be granted, which would defer the pending trials until the next court session in late April. In truth, the continuance was a delaying tactic designed to allow Attorney General John C. Bell the opportunity to petition the Pennsylvania State Supreme Court for a change of venue. The *Record* speculated that if the request was granted the trials would probably move to nearby Lancaster.

Bell's announced intentions surprised defense attorney W.W. MacElree, who represented Denithorne, Keyser and John Conrad. MacElree stated that he would "bitterly oppose" the change of venue petition because there was no evidence that the accused would not receive fair trials in Chester County. "The failure of the commonwealth to win their other cases lies solely in the lack of evidence and the methods pursued," he snarled, not because the citizens of Chester County opposed convictions. Tommy Lack, the other defense attorney in the October trials, publicly supported

MacElree's decision with the declaration that a trial by jury "does not mean a jury composed of men in some other county." West Chester resident Charles V. Echoff sarcastically echoed the sentiments of most people: "If Chester County cannot produce twelve men intelligent enough to try those Coatesville lynching cases, it is time we all moved over to New Jersey or some other state." The consequence of MacElree's opposition would be a legal battle before the state supreme court, and that would take time. Regardless of the outcome, MacElree understood that any delay would give the commonwealth more time to prepare its case against his clients.

On January 31, 1912, as the Chester County Court of Oyer and Terminer opened, a grand jury listened to the evidence against Lewis Denithorne, John Conrad and Lewis Keyser. Then, in a clear and forceful manner, Judge Butler told the jurors, "It is sufficient to say that when a human being is wilfully burned to death by other human beings, murder is committed, and that those who are present at such killing, physically aiding the act, or by word encouraging it, and those who, though absent from the killing, have by deed or word voluntarily aided the movement to slay, are all guilty of some degree of murder." After considering the judge's statement and the evidence against the three young men, the jury ordered them to stand trial for first-degree murder for participating in the lynching of Zachariah Walker. The *West Chester Daily Local News* printed Butler's entire charge to the grand jury and supported his determined attitude to obtain justice in the lynching trials. The *Coatesville Record* merely reported the meeting of the grand jury, neglecting to mention Butler's charge. Having been in jail for three months already, the three defendants faced the prospect of remaining in jail until late April or early May, depending on how quickly the state supreme court acted on Bell's petition.

The commonwealth's request for a continuance was filed in West Chester, and Judge Butler subsequently deferred the remaining trials until the April court session. On February 5, 1912, Bell, Gawthrop and Cunningham presented seven change of venue petitions to the state supreme court in Philadelphia. (The commonwealth did not request that Norman Price's trial be moved, a point that defense attorneys would emphasize in their counterstatement to the supreme court.) Cunningham made a few brief remarks before the justices, essentially summarizing the reasons for the petitions and providing some background information; he also submitted seventy pages of written argument. The supreme court justices agreed to examine the petitions and establish a date for the presentation of counterarguments, if they believed a different point of view was required.

The heart of each petition was that "a fair and impartial trial" in Chester County was impossible because there existed "a well defined, deep seated, deliberately formed and openly expressed public sentiment to the effect that no white man shall be convicted and punished for having participated in the lynching of the colored victim of the mob." This sentiment, the petitions noted, was not confined to Coatesville but permeated the entire county. The petitions concluded with the powerful statement: "On account of the deliberate, notorious and openly expressed purpose of the citizens of that county to condone the murder of the negro…to try the cases now remaining for trial before juries selected from Chester County, would only result in turning the administration of justice into a complete mockery and travesty."

On February 19, 1912, MacElree and Joseph Baldwin, representing the attorneys for the remaining defendants, presented papers to the state supreme court contesting a change of venue. Their opposition rested upon two points: an alleged lack of public sentiment opposing convictions in Chester County, and the constitutional issue of trial by a jury of one's peers. In disputing the commonwealth's assertion that a fair trial was impossible in Chester County, the defense attorneys contended that each jury had reached its verdict based on the evidence presented and that weaknesses in the prosecution's presentations, not citizen bias, had determined the outcomes in those trials.

The defense attorneys' challenge on constitutional grounds was stronger and more important. In arguing that a change of venue would deny the accused a basic constitutional guarantee, they offered a written interpretation of two provisions of the 1874 Pennsylvania Constitution, sections concerning trial by jury, that was significantly different from the commonwealth's argument.

Two days after receiving the petition contesting a change of venue, the Pennsylvania Supreme Court rendered its decision. The justices denied the state's request on the grounds that, in their opinion, the previous trials had been conducted in a fair and impartial manner and the juries had reached their decisions in accordance with the evidence presented. In addition, the court upheld the constitutional objections of the defense. On February 22, the *Record* published a "special night extra edition" to announce the decision and lauded the ruling with the front-page headline, "SUPREME COURT FLATLY

REFUSES CHANGE OF VENUE." William Long explained that the quick decision proved "the position of the Commonwealth in asking for a change of venue was not a strong one" and that the citizens of Chester County, like any other citizens, would render a guilty verdict if the commonwealth could produce evidence conclusively linking the accused to the crime.

Whatever pleasure local residents might have taken in the supreme court's ruling was tempered by the sudden emergence of another crisis in the community. In mid-February a typhoid fever epidemic broke out in Coatesville and the neighboring townships. The disease developed because of an inadequate water supply (tainted wells and a shallow reservoir), the lingering result of rapid population and economic expansion in the community and a reluctance to construct new facilities to keep pace with urban growth. On several occasions in recent years there had been outbreaks of typhoid fever, but only a few people had been stricken, and nothing was done to alleviate the problem. This time, however, within a few days of the first reported case on February 12, several hundred people had contracted the deadly disease. Schools were closed, and the Coatesville Hospital overflowed with patients. An "emergency hospital" was established in the Elks Lodge on East Main Street to accommodate the growing number of sick people, and a corps of visiting nurses was brought in to assist local healthcare workers. A team of experts was dispatched by the Pennsylvania Department of Health to locate the source of the fever and remedy the problem; in addition, they established strict guidelines for drinking water and helped coordinate medical treatment for fever victims.

This latest crisis produced a local reaction that stood in striking contrast to the community's response to the lynching six months earlier. Led by newspaper editor William Long, Coatesville residents demanded to know who was responsible for the typhoid fever epidemic and the neglected water supply, and they joined him in praising the intervention of the state government to end the crisis. When the epidemic waned in March, Long proceeded to launch a surprising campaign against the borough council. He called upon the members to resign as a group, declaring that *they* were ultimately responsible for the epidemic, in light of their control over public utilities. Furthermore, he concluded, the public no longer had any confidence in their leadership. Long also penned a vitriolic editorial in which he cast further blame on the council for neglecting a 1911 Department of Health directive to install a new water treatment facility. He referred to council members as "the water snake gang" for failing to build the new plant because it cost too much. Two editorials followed, exalting the efforts of the Department of Health during the crisis and conceding that "Coatesville at least has learned that there are some good things at Harrisburg that are worthwhile."

With the lynching trials nearly a month away and the typhoid fever epidemic on the wane, Coatesville's attention focused on the Republican Party's 1912 presidential primary. In early April, it was announced that Theodore Roosevelt, campaigning for the nomination against William Howard Taft, would visit Coatesville just prior to the April 14 primary election. The announcement that the former president would give a brief campaign speech in predominantly Republican Coatesville created widespread excitement. On Wednesday, April 10, thousands of people, many of whom the *Record* said "only come to town once in a while," flocked to see "the man," clogging streets, stores, hotels and the train station. It was the largest crowd in the history of Coatesville—larger, in fact, than the crowds at the lynching and at Edgar Rice's funeral—with over six thousand people jammed into the area along Third Avenue and the railroad tracks. The six-man police force and the entire borough council stood with Roosevelt on the reviewing stand. Charles Umsted and Stanley Howe, both indicted for involuntary manslaughter in the lynching, flanked the former president throughout his speech, which lasted only six minutes. Roosevelt was given a "great reception," and the roar of applause and cheers echoed off the surrounding hills for several minutes.

Four days later, Roosevelt carried Coatesville and the surrounding townships of the county and captured a local delegate's vote in the upcoming Republican Party convention. Ironically, just five months earlier, as the first lynching trials opened, the former president had blasted the borough and its leaders for the despicable crime. As a contributing editor to the highly respected national magazine *The Outlook*, Roosevelt had written an article entitled "Lynching and the Miscarriage of Justice," in which he claimed that Coatesville residents had "not the slightest excuse for…condoning the actions of the mob," but since no one attempted to stop the lynching or came forward to testify against the participants, all observers were placed "on a level of criminality with their victim." Despite such strong language, Coatesville residents voted overwhelmingly for Roosevelt in the primary. A particular irony is that Umsted and Howe gladly stood beside the man who had so bitterly condemned them and the other residents of the community.

County newspapers—especially the *Record*, which supported Taft—failed to point out Roosevelt's earlier denunciation of Coatesville.

The approaching court session rekindled public interest in the lynching trials. Stories on the disastrous loss of the *Titanic* shared headlines with the trial preparations, and both the *Record* and the *Daily Local News* gave special attention to the activities of the state police detectives. Sergeant C.B. Cady, who had been in Coatesville since the lynching, headed up the investigation by several plainclothes detectives who searched for new evidence and additional witnesses. In a bizarre twist of events, less than two weeks before the trials were to begin, Sergeant Cady was "expelled" from the investigation headquarters at the Taylor House Hotel for "alleged unseemly conduct." A few days later, he was found dead in a Lancaster boardinghouse. While the official cause of death was heart disease, there were mysterious circumstances to contend with, most notably reports that on several occasions just before his untimely death Cady had tried to buy morphine without a prescription. It was rumored that he had uncovered some new evidence or witnesses for the pending trials but had been unable to convey this information to the authorities. The *Record* noted that "evidence in the cases buried with Cady is troubling the prosecution somewhat." Neither Gawthrop nor Cunningham chose to comment on Cady's death, which made the entire episode all the more mysterious.

Adding to the commonwealth's growing list of problems was the availability of certain key witnesses. Ten days before the trials were scheduled to begin, a list of forty witnesses was drawn up and subpoenas were written for each person to appear in court on behalf of the commonwealth. William Mullin, constable from West Chester, delivered the subpoenas and told each person to arrive at the courthouse on April 30 for the opening trial. Mullin was unable to locate four important witnesses whom, the *Record* observed, the prosecution "wanted badly." The four were: Chester Bostic, who had been acquitted in the October trials, turned state's evidence and then left Coatesville; Joseph Swartz, also acquitted in the October trials, who apparently had moved to Chicago; Calvin Vance, a black worker at the gas company, who was rumored to have returned to the South; and Robert Allison, former chief of the Worth Brothers police force, who had relocated to Reno, Nevada, shortly after the lynching. The prosecution, surely disheartened by Cady's death and the loss of its key witnesses, nonetheless studiously prepared for the next round of trials.

One week before the opening of the county court's April session, officials announced that Judge Joseph Hemphill was too ill to continue his duties (particularly in a lengthy and demanding murder trial) and that Judge William S. Butler would preside over all the remaining cases. Instead of two courtrooms operating simultaneously, as was the normal procedure, each case would be heard in Butler's chamber.

On Thursday morning, May 2, 1912, opening arguments began in *Commonwealth v. Lewis Denithorne*. That afternoon, now special prosecutor Gawthrop presented a descriptive narrative of policeman Edgar Rice's murder and Zachariah Walker's lynching. Gawthrop informed the jury that he would prove that Lewis Denithorne was part of the lynch mob that broke into the hospital and dragged Walker to the funeral pyre. The commonwealth pressed for Denithorne's conviction on the charge of second-degree murder in the hopes that the removal of the death penalty would increase its chances of winning the case. Despite the earlier acquittals, Cunningham, Gawthrop and Sproat were convinced that, based on the evidence that had been presented to the grand jury, they had a very persuasive case against Denithorne.

Several witnesses testified that Denithorne had been part of the mob and had also been on the hospital porch on the night of the lynching. However, the most important component of the commonwealth's case was Denithorne's earlier confession that he had participated in the crime. During the grand jury inquest in September 1911, Denithorne had been called as a witness and, as a result of his statements, was arrested on September 28, six weeks after the lynching. Taken immediately to then District Attorney Gawthrop's office in West Chester, he was interrogated by Robert O. Jeffries, West Chester's police chief and a county detective, and Gawthrop. At Gawthrop's request, Lizzie Hartz, a married woman from Downingtown who was with Denithorne on the night Walker was lynched, attended the session "as a witness." Perhaps the two were more than casual acquaintances, for Denithorne declared, "Don't draw her into this thing. Get pencil and paper and I will tell you my story." After Lizzie Hartz was ushered from the office, Denithorne allegedly confessed that he had entered the hospital, helped remove Walker's straitjacket and assisted in dragging him to the fire—in short, he had done everything but strike the match or throw Walker onto the fire. Gawthrop wrote down the exact wording of the confession because, in his own words, he "could write faster and better than Denithorne." He read the written statement to Denithorne, who concurred that it was "just what he said" and, as if to assert its authenticity, then signed it.

The validity of Denithorne's confession became the critical issue of the trial. Jeffries took the witness stand to describe the interrogation in Gawthrop's office. He said that the questioning had taken several hours (Denithorne signed the confession at about 10:00 p.m.) but that the accused had not been coerced in any way. Jeffries testified that Denithorne's confession had been obtained voluntarily, without threats or intimidation. Since the only other witness to this interrogation was Robert Gawthrop, he was called to take the witness stand despite his role as chief prosecutor—the most recent in a series of uncommon courtroom maneuvers during the lynching trials. Gawthrop corroborated Jeffries's testimony, reaffirming that the confession was valid and had been obtained without force. He then read the entire statement to the jury and offered the document as evidence against Denithorne. At the conclusion of Gawthrop's testimony, the commonwealth rested its case.

Upon hearing this testimony and seeing the signed confession, one prominent Chester County attorney categorized the case against Denithorne as "padlocked and the key thrown away." The defense "has no chance," he reasoned, as it would be "impossible to make a defense" when the accused had willingly signed a confession. Indeed, it seemed at long last that the prosecution would obtain a conviction in the lynching trials. Many courtroom spectators agreed that the jury would have to convict Lewis Denithorne, but W.W. MacElree, whom the West Chester paper referred to as "the adroit and gifted lawyer," had not begun his defense.

MacElree stunned the entire courtroom with his opening defense argument. He launched into a demeaning tirade against his own client that was intended to reveal Denithorne as anything "but a sound, sane man." MacElree denounced Denithorne as "an irresponsible person; a person of unsound mind, on whom nothing could be placed as dependence; a man who thought he was a hypnotist, who could hold all women he met with his eyes." He added that the accused was a "'thing,' a mere bit of humanity, whose confession written or otherwise had no weight; could not be taken as dependable; a man who lied in the grand jury room and again lied in making the confession." Although MacElree never categorized Denithorne as insane, he intended to prove that the man was "weak-minded and silly, and that his reputation for veracity is poor." Numerous witnesses stepped forward to confirm this characterization of Denithorne's unreliability with stories of his unusual behavior and activities. The wily lawyer also tried to instill doubt in the minds of the jury by questioning whether Jeffries and Gawthrop had coerced Denithorne into signing the confession, even as he wondered out loud about the validity of the written statement as Gawthrop had recorded it. In summation, MacElree offered virtually no evidence to refute the charges against his client, and Denithorne never took the witness stand to defend himself or comment on his mental capacity.

Following what the West Chester paper called the defense attorney's "remarkable address to the jury," Jesse Cunningham presented the closing arguments for the commonwealth. "In a vigorous manner," the *Daily Local News* observed, Cunningham "attacked and ridiculed the idea of the defendant being of unsound mind." Speaking for about forty minutes, the deputy attorney general reviewed the facts of the case and stressed Denithorne's admitted role in the lynching, particularly his signed confession. In conclusion, he asked the jury to render a verdict that would "clear the skirts of the State" of the disgraceful crime in Coatesville and Chester County, while reemphasizing that the charge was second-degree murder, not first-degree murder.

It was nearly nine o'clock at night when Cunningham finished his closing comments. Judge Butler gave the jury its charge in a speech that the *Coatesville Record* called "most unfavorable to the prisoner." In reviewing the important evidence, he quoted the law on the issue of second-degree murder charges and told the jurors they must decide if the evidence suggested that Denithorne was "weak-minded." The heart of Butler's charge, however, was once again the principle of "equal responsibility." "Even if the prisoner did not by physical help aid in the crime," the judge declared, "he is as guilty as those that did do the actual work, if he aided in encouragement by word." The jury must simply decide if the accused had participated in this crime. When Butler was finished, the commonwealth asked if the jury could take maps and pictures of Coatesville, as well as Denithorne's signed confession, into the deliberation room to assist them in reaching a verdict. The judge realized this was a ploy to get the signed confession into the hands of the jurors and refused the commonwealth's request. Even though it was nearly ten o'clock, the jury began its deliberations. On its third ballot in less than an hour's time, the twelve men voted unanimously for Denithorne's acquittal.

At eight o'clock the next morning, May 3, Judge Butler called the court into session and asked the jury for its decision. Foreman Thomas Taylor announced the verdict in a loud voice: "Not guilty." Gawthrop and Cunningham, who believed they had secured a conviction in this case, were stunned; Denithorne and MacElree simply smiled. Butler himself was visibly displeased with the decision and in a terse, demanding voice told the jury, "Sit down, gentlemen." The *Record* indicated that the jurist's tone "forbode something unusual." In an uncharacteristic action, Butler issued a curt commentary that explicitly denounced the jury's verdict: "Gentlemen, I do not wish to criticize your verdict, but I must say that I regard it as a public calamity and against law and order. The Commonwealth had absolutely proved the guilt of this man and the defense had not offered the slightest bit of evidence as to his innocence, the prisoner not even going on the stand himself. This is all I have to say." Butler promptly dismissed the jurors, several of whom were "furious" with "the harsh words of the Court." Lewis Denithorne was immediately discharged from police custody and left the courtroom with several friends.

Despite the startling verdict, in a matter-of-fact manner the bailiff immediately began preparations for the next lynching trial, *Commonwealth v. Lewis Keyser*. Following jury selection, but before the trial could actually get underway, Robert Gawthrop, speaking for the prosecution, rose to address the court. His comments revealed the commonwealth's almost continuous frustration in investigating the case and the futility of trying the alleged lynchers. Gawthrop simply conceded, "The Commonwealth has now arrived at the point in the Coatesville lynching cases where she feels that it is absolutely impossible for her to secure any convictions in any of the cases."

Having just lost its strongest case, the prosecution capitulated and refused to continue the trials. To pursue convictions against the remaining seven defendants, including Chief of Police Charles Umsted, would, in Gawthrop's opinion, "only tend to humiliate the administration of justice." Instead, he announced that the commonwealth would "submit reluctantly to the results acquired at the hands of the juries," and he asked that the remaining cases be brought before a jury and a verdict of "not guilty" be rendered in each case. Deputy Attorney General Cunningham reiterated Gawthrop's concession with a brief statement acknowledging that all the authorities had performed their full duty and that the commonwealth was "free from any responsibility in the present situation." The failure of justice in these cases, he emphasized, "must necessarily rest with the juries." This was a difficult moment for both Gawthrop and Cunningham, one they had sought to avoid for almost nine months.

Judge William Butler responded to the commonwealth's request with a lengthy, eloquent disquisition on the failure of justice in Chester County. "It certainly is a very sad situation in which we find ourselves," he began. "I do not say it in the spirit of criticism of anybody, but I do say…from what I hear and what I have seen, that there is…a sentiment in this county, a general sentiment, utterly opposed to the prosecution of anybody and of everybody who took part in this horrible affair." When the crime first occurred, he believed that a fair trial for the accused would be difficult but not impossible, given the violent nature of the crime. "The sense of decency of the people would be so outraged by this awful humiliation put upon them," the judge surmised, "that we could not probably get a jury of twelve men in the community who would be competent to justly try the accused." In truth, Butler's fear was the exact opposite of what had transpired in Chester County. "Now I am absolutely convinced," he continued, "that it is impossible to get twelve men in this county…who could, no matter what the evidence is, bring themselves to convict anybody who was connected with this offense. I repeat, I do not say that in criticism, I say it in sorrow."

Butler reiterated that he did not intend to criticize the juries' verdicts but rather "the circumstances that they manifestly did not consider the evidence. They had no time to consider it. They rendered those verdicts, as a rule, inside of minutes, not hours." A normal jury, he declared, would "devote hours, if not days," to a careful review of the evidence before reaching a decision. But the juries in the lynching trials had not been normal. They had carried out their duties with little regard for the solemn nature of their responsibility. The acquittals had come, Butler concluded, because the juries were "evidently controlled by an irresistible, overruling belief and sentiment that there ought to be no conviction." In essence, the verdicts had been reached before the trials began.

Turning his attention to the Denithorne trial, Judge Butler denounced the jury *and* its decision. "In my opinion," he said, "the evidence was an absolute demonstration of this defendant's guilt. There was substantially nothing presented in the way of answer. The defendant did not even take the trouble to go on the stand and say he was not guilty." And yet, because of the strong sentiment opposing convictions, the jurors could have given their decision without deliberation since they were "practically ready to render a verdict of acquittal before [leaving the courtroom]." Butler was convinced that "the action of this jury, in the face of absolutely convincing proof of guilt…is an absolute demonstration that the Commonwealth was justified in saying to our Supreme Court that this sentiment existed, and that a conviction could not be had here." He therefore concurred with the commonwealth's decision to submit the remaining cases to a jury and request verdicts of "not guilty." To continue the trials, "even assuming that the evidence in the remaining cases would be as strong as in the case we just tried," the judge warned, "would simply be to invite certain defeat of the attempt to administer justice." Given the circumstances of a strong anticonviction sentiment and the previous verdicts, Butler concluded, to persist in prosecution would "further demonstrate the powerlessness of the Court and invite increased contempt for the law." He shared the prosecution's frustration that justice could not be served and agreed to the "propriety of abandoning the remaining cases."

The twelve jurymen assembled for Lewis Keyser's trial became the last jury in the lynching cases. The distinguishing feature of this jury was that one of its members was from Coatesville and another was black. This was also the jury that would render verdicts in each of the seven outstanding cases, since a determination of the guilt or innocence of Charles Umsted, Stanley Howe, Richard Tucker, Walter Markward, John Conrad, Lewis Keyser and Norman Price had to be made before the cases could be removed from the docket. Almost as a formality, Judge Butler swore in the jury, and the chief prosecutor declined to offer any evidence against the seven defendants. The jury was then instructed to render verdicts of "not guilty" in each of the cases and in short order did just that. The entire proceedings, the mass acquittal, took less than fifteen minutes and brought to an abrupt end the nine-month ordeal surrounding the lynching of Zachariah Walker. The seven defendants were discharged, and in a scene familiar to those who had followed the trials, friends and well-wishers crowded into the courtroom to offer their congratulations.

Public reaction to the conclusion of the trials was predictably mixed. In a paragraph buried deep in an article that recounted verbatim Butler's discourse, the *Coatesville Record* noted: "The lynching of Zach Walker, the man who murdered Police Officer Edgar Rice, today becomes only a matter of history. The trials are over. Everybody arrested in connection with the crime has been adjudged Not Guilty." Outside the courthouse, the accused men responded joyously to the news of their acquittal. Friends met Lewis Keyser and John Conrad in West Chester and "hailed them with cheers."

In Coatesville, there were no public celebrations and only a few people discussed the verdicts on the streets, in marked contrast to the joyous receptions

A Coatesville steel mill, circa 1910. *Courtesy of the Chester County Historical Society.*

that had heralded the end of each of the October trials. The *Record* reported that Police Chief Umsted was overcome with emotion when he received the news of his freedom, and "tears came to the eyes of the big man." The paper also noted that "Stanley Howe was perhaps the most jubilant of all" when he learned of the acquittals, while Richard Tucker and Walter Markward "took the news as a matter of course," having claimed all along that they had not had anything to do with the lynching and were "victims of circumstance." Many residents accepted the verdicts blandly: "Just as I thought" and "Well, that suits me" were common statements. When asked about the trials, defense attorney W.W. MacElree, whom the *Record* credited with "starting the sentiment for acquittals in the freeing of the boy Schwartz [*sic*]," simply replied: "We have all worked hard. The prosecuting attorneys have had their troubles naturally, but to my mind, fate has had something to with this." He ended with a resounding statement that many people in Chester County, and particularly in Coatesville, either thought privately or said publicly: "There is little to say except we are glad of the finish."

When asked for comment, Pennsylvania's deputy attorney general replied, "No use of arguing or talking of this thing any longer. Let's talk about the weather." Robert Gawthrop's only public comment was that he "had but done the duty of any man in the same position." Ironically, at the seventeenth annual meeting of the Afro-American League of Pennsylvania, a resolution praising the efforts of the state and the attorney general's office for pursuing convictions in the lynching cases was passed on the very day the trials concluded.

Beyond Coatesville and Chester County there was an almost universal condemnation of the acquittals. Some Pennsylvania newspapers were particularly vehement in their denunciations, since the outcome reflected on the entire state, and almost all of them specifically recalled the tragedy and noted the failure of justice. The *Philadelphia Press* referred to "a most regrettable end," while the *Johnstown Leader* called the acquittals "a disgrace to Pennsylvania." The *Philadelphia Bulletin* was most emphatic in its editorial headlined "COATESVILLE'S FINAL SHAME," declaring that there had been "an entire failure of justice" and that the acquittals indicated "Chester County justifies, or at least condones," mob violence. The *Pittsburgh Courier*, a black newspaper, lamented that the lynching had brought "shame and disgrace" to Pennsylvania. "There is no escaping the shame," the editors noted. "The whole state must shoulder the curse." The *Harrisburg Telegraph* expressed the final tragedy in its headline "LYNCHERS OF WALKER WILL GO UNPUNISHED." Amid this barrage of anti-acquittal editorials and headlines, the *Coatesville Record* and *West Chester Daily Local News* offered no rebuttals. In fact, neither newspaper ran an editorial about the trials or their results. The most succinct comment was the simple opening sentence of the *Record*'s article announcing the acquittals: "The lynching cases are at an end." Indeed, they were.

In the weeks that followed, Chester County newspapers remarked on the cost of the trials, with the *Record* estimating the total expense for county taxpayers at $25,000.00. According to the *Daily Local News*, "That lynchings in a county are more of a luxury than a necessity is attested to by the fact that it cost the county of Chester just $10,406.40 to conduct the investigation and trials of those who were supposed to have been implicated in the Coatesville affair." Perhaps the expense of the investigation and trials would somehow "cause some of those in power to give more determined efforts to prevent a repetition of [such a] crime." Although the difference between the *Record*'s estimate and the actual cost (as reported in the *Daily Local News*) was large, the Coatesville lynching affair was still the most costly legal proceedings in the history of Pennsylvania up to that time.

By August, Coatesville and its mills were in the midst of an economic revival, and local residents seemed determined not to dwell on the upcoming first anniversary of the lynching. On August 13, 1912, this single sentence was buried on the last page of the *Record*: "Just one year tonight from the date of the most deplorable incident in Coatesville's history, but in spite of all her traducers, the town is bigger and better than ever." The *Daily Local News* published a two-sentence reminder of the episode deep inside the paper, without benefit of a headline. "Fresh in the minds of some," the paper observed, "most people, however, have forgotten the terrible crime."

One individual did not want the tragedy to be forgotten. John Jay Chapman, a New York essayist and "crusader" who had followed the entire affair with great interest and had brooded over it, journeyed to Coatesville on the first anniversary of the lynching. He advertised a community prayer meeting, hoping that area residents would attend and atone for the "dreadful crime." The *Daily Local News* observed that most people were "weary of the lynching case," but Chapman was undaunted. He scheduled the meeting for Sunday, August 18, in a rented storeroom (the Nagle Building) in downtown Coatesville. Only two people—a visitor to Coatesville and a black woman from nearby Hayti whom Chapman believed "was a spy sent to see what was going on"— joined Chapman and his wife. Despite the minuscule turnout, Chapman delivered a powerful and persuasive speech in which he blamed the Coatesville lynching on slavery. He referred to the incident as an American tragedy, part of the national corruption and evil that permeated the American character, and insisted that all Americans were responsible for Zachariah Walker's death. The only way to resolve the evil, Chapman insisted, was through national penance. At the conclusion of the prayer meeting, Chapman delivered a copy of his address to the *Record* office. William Long published the entire speech on the front page of the paper but offered no editorial comment, other than to state that it had been well prepared and contained "no objectionable features." Chapman's "Coatesville Address" was reprinted in several periodicals and newspapers, including *Harper's Weekly*, and it also appeared later in pamphlet form and in a collection of his writings. Coatesville residents may have chosen to forget the lynching, but its legacy would continue to haunt the community. The entire episode had been a tragedy for Coatesville and, as Chapman said, a tragedy for the nation as well.

Chapter 5
"AN AMERICAN TRAGEDY"

Early on Monday morning, August 14, 1911, as young boys sold souvenir bone fragments on Main Street, Walter Greenwood entered his downtown Coatesville law office. He was greeted with a telegram from H.W. Wheatly, a Washington, D.C. attorney and friend. "Dear Walter," the message read. "Congratulations! Coatesville is now a Southern city." The irony of the remark was not lost on Greenwood nor on his son, who told this story seventy-five years after the fact. Lynchings, everyone knew, were something that happened in the South; they were a *southern* problem, as was the so-called race question in general. Still, one of the most heinous and highly publicized lynchings of the era had just occurred in the North, and in a Pennsylvania steel town. Given that Coatesville embodied the material progress that was to lead the country into a new era of human potential and accomplishment, was the lynching of Zachariah Walker an aberration, an accident of history, or was it somehow tied to the very meaning of "progress"? In light of the seventy other lynchings that occurred in America that year, and the more than thirty-five hundred at the turn of the century, could history and progress in America continue to be judged as synonymous?

As the subsequent investigation and prosecutions showed, the lynching of Walker was not an accident; nor was it a spontaneous act, the product of impulse. Despite the early characterizations of events on "that quiet Sabbath evening," in time it became clear that the murder of the black steelworker had been perpetrated by men and boys with close ties to the

The first railroad bridge across the Brandywine Creek, with Coatesville in the background, circa 1857. *Courtesy of the Lukens Archives and the Chester County Historical Society.*

community. As Walker was brought into the police lockup that Sunday afternoon, a local man yelled to the waiting crowd, "That man ought to be lynched!" and later that day his recommendation was acted upon. For several hours, word of the impending deed had passed from lip to lip, and people from neighboring communities flooded into Coatesville to witness the event. By its utter silence, a crowd of several thousand spectators voiced its approval of the horrible crime. Although the newspapers and borough officials maintained that the abduction and lynching had occurred outside the town boundary, thereby absolving the residents of blame, the weight of evidence suggested otherwise. Walker's death was planned and initiated on the streets of Coatesville and was purposely staged outside the town limits to safeguard those involved.

Although bystanders at Newlin's farm that evening watched the lynching with morbid curiosity, with the exception of some teenage boys near the fire, the crowd was, by every account, polite and well mannered. Men stood aside so women and children could have a more advantageous view of the victim as he struggled to free himself and escape the flames, his flesh smoldering and his body racked with unimaginable pain. No one objected as three times Walker was clubbed and thrown back onto the pyre. As was the custom, people waited hours for the ashes to cool so that relics could be picked up.

One boy even carried Walker's finger in his pants pocket for six weeks, although his father had vehemently objected when the child was presented with the souvenir by a family friend. The Commonwealth of Pennsylvania devoted nearly ten months and $10,000 to the prosecution of those suspected of killing Walker, but the resolve of the community to protect the instigators proved too strong for county and state authorities.

Any effort to understand the lynching of Zachariah Walker, or any such episode of mass violence, involves an assessment of social circumstances—the realities of time and place—and the personal motivations of the participants. The Coatesville lynching was an extraordinary event, but one that was intimately tied to the everyday life of ordinary people in a northern steel town. As such, an examination of this horrible episode can shed light on the nature of lynching at the turn of the century, the process of social change and adjustment in industrializing America and the way in which communities react to instances of crisis. Walker's demise that Sunday evening, and the very manner of his death, was not unrelated to the social setting in which the crime was perpetrated. Social circumstances clearly fused with a prevailing psychology in an act of collective vengeance that was striking in its finality. Such circumstances "predisposed individuals to find martyrs," Elliott Gorn has noted, but they also created a separate cast of heroes and villains. Given the reigning psychology—the siege mentality that existed following Edgar Rice's death—those same individuals were capable of enormous self-deception long after the lynching had occurred. For reasons he may not have appreciated entirely, John Jay Chapman was correct when he called the lynching of Zachariah Walker an "American tragedy."

To intimate that the events surrounding Walker's death were directly related to the web of community relations that existed in Coatesville in 1911 is not to suggest that social conditions caused so terrible a scene to be enacted. However, the lynching did occur in a social milieu quite different from that of most, if not all, other lynchings during the era. Therefore, to appreciate the real and symbolic meaning of the tragedy, to understand more completely something of the participants and their world at a particular moment in time, it is necessary to consider the nature of black-white relations in Coatesville and the events of August 13 in the context of broader patterns of community life. Conventional interpretations of lynching seem inadequate in assessing the dynamics of overlapping group relationships in this northern industrial town. However, the application of social theory to this concrete historical event provides a useful framework in which to consider the importance of Walker's death and the character of race relations in Coatesville.

In his influential study of social deviance in seventeenth-century New England, sociologist Kai Erikson developed the theory of "boundary maintenance" to explain how communities react to defiance of the shared system of values and beliefs on which the social order is predicated. Erikson built on the earlier work of Emile Durkheim, who was concerned with the extent to which a society would go to preserve order and stability. Durkheim argued in *The Division of Labor in Society* that there was a close connection between criminality, deviant behavior and what he termed "repressive justice." In punishing acts of social defiance, a society, which Durkheim referred to as a "collective conscience," shows its displeasure with the criminal and reaffirms the consensus on which harmony is based. As it makes such judgments, a society delineates the limits of acceptable conduct. Durkheim noted that the more serious the perceived threat to society (and its self-defined norms), the more repressive the punishment inflicted by agents who are sanctioned by the larger group.

Drawing upon Durkheim's insight, Erikson formulated the theory of boundary maintenance to explain how communities react to defiance of the shared system of values and beliefs. In any localized society, there is an accepted pattern of relationships, a sense of "communality" that gives to each member and group a place in the larger social structure. Traditionally, these relationships are defined by law *and* by custom. This sense of community, or communality, is, in Erikson's words, a state of mind based on a "network of understandings" that has endured over time. "The deviant," according to Erikson, "is a person whose activities have moved outside the margins of the group, and when the community calls him to account for that vagrancy it is making a statement about the nature and placement of its boundaries." The issue of acceptable conduct is clearly related to that of power and authority, but it is also intimately tied to the shared values of the community. It is possible for a person to be within the law but to have transgressed the custom(s) of a community—in Erikson's words, to have threatened its integrity. Single encounters between a deviant and the society must be judged as "only fragments of an ongoing social process."

Punishment, an act of repressive justice, is intended to return the offender to the fold or else, to use Durkheim's expression, to "expiate" the deviant.

By such actions, a society is both defended and avenged. Durkheim and Erikson recognized that there are moments of social crisis when members of the group find that mere penal sanctions, a recourse to the courts and adherence to due process for satisfaction, are inadequate to the occasion. Given the nature of the challenge, moderation simply will not suffice. In such instances, repressive justice is an extreme, though socially acceptable, mechanism of restitution, or boundary maintenance. Such measures may not be within the framework of the law, but they may nonetheless receive the approval of the community, which in turn allows the perpetrators to go unpunished. Acts of repressive justice are intended to restore law and order by circumventing legal institutions when necessary.

In the summer of 1911, Coatesville was a community caught up in history, a community immersed in the broad pattern of social and economic reorganization that characterized much of the rest of the nation in the early twentieth century. In many respects, Coatesville was also a community in the throes of a boundary crisis, much as Erikson thought was the case in Salem Village more than two centuries earlier. Such a view allows for the widest possible latitude in understanding the lynching of Zachariah Walker, as well as what followed during the next nine months. Within a single generation at the turn of the century, Coatesville experienced a demographic transformation of unprecedented scope that challenged the

A view of Lukens Steel and the viaduct bridge, circa 1911. *Courtesy of the Chester County Historical Society.*

very meaning of *community* for longtime residents of the borough. The abrupt changes that attended the rapid reorganization of life in this localized society demanded considerable physical and psychological adjustments by the native inhabitants, not the least of which was contending with new population groups, the harbingers of change. Although residents did not realize it, or would not admit it to themselves, the very engines of material progress did much to undermine social stability and in the end led to the crisis of August 13, 1911. By lynching Zachariah Walker, the citizens of Coatesville were not only making a statement about the acceptable limits of conduct—that is, the nature of community boundaries—but they were, in their own fashion, coming to terms with history.

Although it always had other manufacturing concerns, Coatesville was (and remains) a steel town. An appreciation of the importance of the two steel mills—Worth Brothers and Lukens—to the local economy and culture helps to explain the circumstances behind the borough's rapid development into the early twentieth century. The companies fueled the local economy and were the font of prosperity for residents. As with Steelton, Johnstown and numerous communities surrounding Pittsburgh, the fortunes of Coatesville were linked to the success of the mills. The Worth Brothers and Lukens mills, like other iron- and steelworks throughout Pennsylvania, dramatically increased their production capabilities in the first years of the twentieth century so as to exploit expanding markets. Both companies built new plate mills in 1902–3, each wider than any other in the United States; and, at the same time, each firm acquired new holdings in other states. While Worth Brothers provided its own pig iron, Lukens took control of several companies in Virginia, which gave it easy access to needed raw materials. Later in the decade, as the two companies began to recover from the economic panic of 1907, new blast furnaces were opened at each of the several mill sites in Coatesville. During the summer of 1911, for the first time in four years, the local mills operated at nearly full capacity.

In Pennsylvania, steel production grew nearly 90 percent in the first decade of the twentieth century as technological innovations revolutionized the industry. Steel towns across the commonwealth registered significant increases in population during this same period, due in large part to requisite adjustments in the nature of labor skills in the iron and steel industries. More and more, a premium was placed on semiskilled and

Headquarters of the Lukens Steel Company, from a postcard marked 1911. *Courtesy of the Chester County Historical Society.*

unskilled laborers who were willing to work long hours for relatively low wages. Fluctuations in the economy during the decade, which hit the steel industry especially hard, only accelerated the trend toward hiring additional workers at lower hourly wages. In Coatesville, the physical expansion of the Worth Brothers and Lukens mills necessitated the recruitment of a large number of laborers. As was the custom in the industry, they both employed contractors and labor agents to locate available workers and transport them to Coatesville.

In addition to hiring local men and teenage boys, the companies drew on two other pools of potential workers: immigrants and southern blacks. With increasing regularity after 1903, company agents met European immigrants as they arrived at Atlantic Coast seaports and contracted their labor for the mills in Coatesville. They also recruited a growing number of black laborers from Virginia and the southern Atlantic region of the United States. In his report on industrial development in 1911, the Pennsylvania secretary of internal affairs noted the latter trend and predicted that, as a result of their employment in steel mills in the commonwealth, "the future will bring greatly improved conditions for this class of people." Unlike Pittsburgh and steel towns in the western part of the state, where immigrants and blacks were recruited as strikebreakers or as replacement workers for disgruntled native white employees, there is no evidence that this was the case in Coatesville. Rather, by the end of the decade the steel mills in Coatesville were committed to hiring greater numbers of laborers from outside the state based on their willingness to accept modest wages for long hours of difficult work. The presence of these newcomers also had potentially harmful consequences for social relationships in the town.

Between 1890 and 1920, the physical expansion of Coatesville was judged to be but one measure of the improvement in the lives of its residents. Signs of the material progress brought by the mills were seen up and down Main Street in the multiplication of new stores, taverns and hotels and in the increased number of middle- and upper-middle-class residences built beyond Third Avenue. By 1911, there was even a building boom in neighboring Valley Township, an area near the mills known as Valley View. New churches and schools were constructed, and the growing number of social clubs and fraternal associations attested to the comfort of community life. Town boosterism was particularly strong. In the summer of 1911, civic

A civic parade on Main Street, Coatesville. *Courtesy of the Frank Pennegar Collection and the Chester County Historical Society.*

leaders celebrated the outdoor electrification of the downtown business district by dubbing Main Street the "White Way." The Business Men's Association plaque placed in the new park eleven months after Zachariah Walker's death called Coatesville "an ideal town for home and industry." Two longtime residents who recalled these years, the years of their childhood, remembered a close-knit community, a "family place."

The period of greatest change and adjustment in Coatesville was from 1900 to 1910, the decade preceding the lynching. As the town's reputation grew, and as labor agents recruited new workers from beyond Chester County, new population groups arrived in steadily increasing numbers. United States census records for that decade indicate what was happening in the community (see table, following). Between 1890 and 1900, the number of people living in the Borough of Coatesville increased by 55 percent. Nearly 88 percent of the residents in 1900 were classified as native white; 4.8 percent were foreign-born; and the remaining 7.5 percent were Negro, the vast majority of whom had been born in Pennsylvania. As might be expected, the substantially larger native white population dominated the political, economic and social life of the borough. By 1910, however, the census records reveal a very different milieu. Especially after 1903, Coatesville experienced a sudden and sustained increase in its foreign-born and black populations that was strikingly out of proportion to the increase in the native white population. The total population of the borough in 1910 was nearly double that of 1900 and more than three times the number of inhabitants registered in 1890. (In the same twenty-year period, the population of Chester County increased by only 22 percent; the population of Pennsylvania, by 46 percent.) The native white population of Coatesville in 1910 showed an increase in absolute numbers but a relative decline to 73 percent of the total population. Foreign-born inhabitants now constituted 13.3 percent of the population and were more than five times as numerous as they had been just ten years earlier. The black population of the borough also experienced a significant increase greater than any other municipality in Pennsylvania—from less than 8 to nearly 14 percent of the total number of inhabitants. Foreign-born and black residents of Coatesville in 1910 thus constituted over one-quarter of the total population, and it should be noted that some 70 percent of the newcomers were male.

BOROUGH OF COATESVILLE POPULATION, 1890–1920

YEAR	TOTAL	NATIVE WHITE[1]	FOREIGN-BORN	NEGRO
1890	3,679	3,200 (87%)	161 (4.4%)	318 (8.6%)
1900	5,721	5,017 (87.7%)	273 (4.8%)	431 (7.5%)
1910	11,082[2]	8,093 (73%)	1,469 (13.3%)	1,520[3] (13.7%)
1920	14,514	10,882 (75%)	1,751 (12%)	1,881 (13%)

Source: U.S. Census, 1890–1920

[1] The native white population includes all whites born in the United States, whether one, both or neither parents is foreign-born.

[2] In 1910, there were 2,189 dwelling places in the borough and 2,276 families listed in the census.

[3] There were only two "colored" inhabitants of the borough in 1910 (meaning Indian or Oriental).

The explanation for this significant decade-long demographic shift is twofold. Coatesville, a community in the heartland of southeastern Pennsylvania, experienced the brunt of both the so-called New Immigration

A view of the Pennsylvania Railroad bridge spanning the Brandywine Creek at Coatesville. *Courtesy of the Chester County Historical Society.*

(of European immigrants) and the migration of blacks from the American South, both in response to the economic opportunities the steel mills offered. In 1910, the largest number of foreign-born inhabitants of the borough were from southern and eastern Europe, with Poles (the largest group), Russians, Austrians and Italians making up over 60 percent of the local immigrant population. Of the newly arrived black inhabitants in 1910, the greatest number were from Virginia and Maryland.

Students of American history are familiar with the massive immigration of southern and eastern Europeans to this country at the turn of the century. In all, more than twenty-five million foreigners arrived in the half century following the Civil War, lured by the promise of a better life in the industrializing cities. These newcomers transplanted their cultures in American soil, retaining traditional habits and beliefs as they sought their place in society. During these same years, a growing number of blacks left the South in an effort to escape the racial prejudices and economic deprivation that followed in the wake of emancipation. "Following the North Star" became a popular expression for some million and a half black migrants in the years before World War I. Most historians of the black migration emphasize the importance of labor shortages as an explanation for the arrival in the North of several million more southern blacks between 1916 and the eve of World War II. In her novel *Jonah's Gourd Vine*, Zora Neale Hurston captured the ambivalence of those blacks who traveled north seeking opportunity and deliverance. "And black men's feet learned roads," she wrote. "Some said goodbye cheerfully... others fearfully, with terrors of unknown dangers in their mouths...others in their eagerness for distance said nothing. The daybreak found them gone. The wind said North. Trains said North. The tides and tongues said North, and men moved like the great herds before the glacier." For all of the migrants, but especially the southern blacks, their reception was not always what they expected, and the deliverance they sought was not as apparent as they might have hoped.

By 1911, Coatesville had earned the reputation as a place where jobs were available, particularly for anyone willing to work sixty hours a week at $0.14 to $0.15 an hour. One newspaper account from the period celebrated the success of a company agent operating in Norfolk, Virginia, who was able to secure one hundred foreign and black laborers and transport them directly to Coatesville on a special car provided by the Pennsylvania Railroad. These men were put to work on the morning they arrived in town at what was then considered a generous wage of $1.50 a day. Worth Brothers paid their railroad fares and arranged for the men to find housing. By 1911, an informal network of contacts had developed between Coatesville and areas of Virginia where company agents were active, and whether through the enticement of labor agents or through knowledge of the community from neighbors and relatives, a steady stream of southern blacks found their way to the borough. That Coatesville was situated some twenty miles north of Pennsylvania's border with Maryland and Delaware and was easily reached by rail further encouraged black men to relocate there. A highly critical editorial printed in the *Coatesville Record* seven months before the lynching acknowledged the borough's popularity with black migrants. "Coatesville has for years been the Mecca for negroes from the Southern towns," editor William Long wrote, "whose former places of residence have [been] made too hot for them." After the lynching, William Diggs, a local black man, former borough police officer and one of the numerous agents who operated for the steel companies in Virginia and Maryland, found that potential laborers in these states had heard of the incident but were not discouraged from coming to Coatesville.

In Coatesville, the established residents of both races only grudgingly accepted the newcomers. Their desire to assimilate the strangers into the established order and at the same time keep them at bay created conflicting loyalties that were not easily resolved. Although there were no Jim Crow ordinances or other formal mechanisms of social segregation in Coatesville, a discernible pattern of racial and ethnic separation existed on the eve of the Walker lynching. Such a pattern was not the product of accident or chance but of a conscious desire to control the newcomers and assure the maintenance of established customs and relationships within the community. This isolation exaggerated the view of newcomers as malcontents and degenerates, as outsiders who posed a threat by their very presence.

On the eve of the lynching, there was little residential integration in Coatesville. The established native white and native black neighborhoods existed side by side but with distinct boundaries that were not crossed. Many of the long-standing black families in the borough were said to be descendants of an earlier generation of migrants from the South, those men and women who had journeyed north on the Underground Railroad in the years preceding the Civil War. By the early twentieth century, they were firmly established in the community, mostly residing in an area north of

The stone arched bridge that crossed the flats near Lukens Steel, circa 1904. *Courtesy of the Chester County Historical Society.*

Main Street between Sixth and Eighth Avenues known as the "East End" or the "Eighties." The native white community surrounded area blacks on three sides (to the north were the tracks of the Pennsylvania Railroad), with neighborhoods characterized more by income and social status than by any other factors. A few blacks lived in white neighborhoods, usually because they were employed as domestic servants. This pattern of residential housing was the result of custom and reinforced the long-standing practice of restricted social contacts between the races. It is worth noting that, although there seemed to be an understanding among local whites and blacks regarding racial etiquette, throughout 1911 the newspapers carried reports of gangs of white and black youths in the old neighborhoods. Despite verbal confrontations, there were no serious instances of violence.

As the population of the borough grew, the established pattern of separation held but added some new features. Neither the native whites nor the native blacks welcomed the newcomers into the settled neighborhoods.

"Foreigners" from Europe and from the South were forced to seek housing away from the center of town. As was the custom in other cities and industrial towns across America, each ethnic group tended to cluster with its own kind, and in the case of Coatesville, this meant that newcomers settled on the periphery of the borough proper. What quickly emerged were blocks, streets and patches of lower-income housing associated with their ethnic and racial occupants. The two steel companies strengthened this pattern of geographic isolation by offering cheap, poorly maintained company housing well off the beaten path, a practice that enhanced the image of the newcomers as outsiders.

Towering over the landscape of Coatesville were the Lukens and Worth Brothers mills, situated on the banks of the Brandywine Creek in an industrial valley that ran on a north–south axis west of First Avenue. Russians, Ukrainians, Austrians, Poles and Italians settled west of the mills in an area of working-class houses known as the "West End." To the north, in a hilly area above town, was Rock Run, where Europeans and some southern

A view of Lukens Steel standing on the railroad bridge and looking south. *Courtesy of the Chester County Historical Society.*

blacks congregated, many of them in company-owned houses and shacks. Although it had always been considered part of Coatesville, Rock Run was in Valley Township and therefore technically outside the borough limits. The remnants of an old Pennock ironworks were still visible in 1911, and a woolen mill continued to operate in the vicinity. In the years immediately following the Civil War, Irish immigrants settled along the creek, giving the area's main access road the nickname "Irish Lane." The southern black migrants who arrived in the area ten months after the lynching were supplied with materials to fix up their dwellings in Rock Run, bought for them by the steel companies from downtown merchants.

A third area where newly arrived workers settled or were placed was the Spruces. Situated high on South Hill overlooking the industrial valley and Coatesville to the north, the Spruces was just beyond the southern borough boundary in East Fallowfield Township. Most of the residents of the area's small houses and shacks were employed at the main Worth Brothers mill, which was within walking distance. Below the Spruces on Youngsburg Road was Bernardtown, with stores and taverns that catered chiefly to blacks and immigrants. During the first decade of the twentieth century, the population of the township, which consisted chiefly of farm families, increased more than 40 percent, mainly due to the rise in the number of inhabitants of the Spruces and Bernardtown.

Rock Run, the Spruces and Bernardtown were all at least one mile from the shops and taverns on East Main Street in Coatesville, and easy access to the commercial district was all but impossible in the absence of public transportation. Because there were no public streetlights in the outlying districts, it was treacherous passage, especially from Rock Run, along the blackened roads and across the several bridges once nightfall came. There was also the custom that immigrants and blacks did not drink in the established saloons that catered to the native white population. Consequently, the newcomers were more likely to take their trade to stores and taverns closer to their dwelling places. Weekend displays of public drunkenness and bravado were frequent, not only along Main Street, but more so in Rock Run and the Spruces. These working-class districts, where bootleg alcohol regularly fueled the inhabitants' passions, were known throughout the county as tough, violent dens of misdeeds. Only rarely did the Monday edition of the *Coatesville Record* not report some mischievous weekend incident that had called the police to Rock Run or the Spruces. On Saturday evening, August

12, Zachariah Walker had been on his way home to the Spruces, primed with the rewards of the day's fellowship in a local tavern, when he came upon Edgar Rice at the foot of South Hill.

Even before Zachariah Walker arrived in Coatesville, local citizens resented the European immigrants and southern blacks who were present in the borough, and the passage of time, accompanied by an increase in the number of newcomers, seemed to exacerbate those tensions. Residents believed that because these "foreigners," or "aliens," were unwilling to accept the established ways of the community, they were undermining the fabric of social stability. News of "trouble" in the newcomers' settlements on the edge of town had become commonplace, and what appeared to residents to be a mounting wave of violent crime, crimes against persons and property, served to validate their perception of blacks and immigrants as destroyers of harmony and order. Men, both natives and newcomers, had taken to carrying concealed weapons, in violation of the law. Residents saw this pattern of violence, fueled by the presence of alcohol, as a sign of the

Brandywine Mansion, once the home of matriarch and mill operator Rebecca Lukens and today a historic site. *Courtesy of the Lukens Archives and the Chester County Historical Society.*

general disintegration of civility, and they placed the blame squarely on the shoulders of the borough's recent arrivals.

Newspaper accounts as well as court records show that a disproportionate number of cases brought before magistrates in West Chester involved defendants from Coatesville, and a high percentage of these involved foreign immigrants and newly arrived blacks. In mid-September 1910, for example, a family of four was brutally murdered in Coatesville, and a young Polish resident who could not speak English was arrested for the crime. On September 22, the day following his arrest, the *Record* printed a revealing editorial on the incident, one that foreshadowed the prevailing wisdom a year later:

> *Murder, the willful taking of a life, is terrible in itself…although murder in itself is too often lacking of the proper punishment.*
>
> *If there is a just punishment for such a crime it should be meted out hastily. There should be no quibbling of justice; there should be no more delay than is actually necessary and that necessity should not be a minute of lost time.*
>
> *Law is law, but law is not always justice. The law may cause delay. If it does, it does no justice to the county, nor to a country in which there are entirely new crimes perpetuated by foreign elements.*
>
> *We do not advocate mob rule. Lynchings are deplored but too often are they caused by a lack of faith in the court. The courts of Chester County are among the best in the country. Lynchings in this county are not on record, but even this court can now make a distinction for hastening proper justice and punishment.*

If convicted, the *Record* declared, "that fiend" should be executed by hanging without delay. Unfortunately, the paper neglected to inform its readers that the suspect had already been released.

Ironically, native inhabitants of Coatesville denounced the unwillingness of the European immigrants and southern blacks to conform to the established norm, yet they were not quite sure that they wanted to fully assimilate these people into the social and political structure of the community. The *Record* acknowledged the conflicting social agenda in a March 1911 commentary entitled "Foreigners and Revolvers":

*Our population is becoming every day more cosmopolitan, and the intricacies
therefore increasing. Perhaps the question of just what we intend to do with
these people is not as vital as* [what] *they might do to us. Some of the
social customs brought from European shores threaten to overthrow some of
our cherished institutions and our easy-going Americans here give very little
thought to the possibilities that lie in this fact.*

What will [be] *the influence of these foreign born people upon our
politics when they become citizens is only conjecture. How will the customs
that are strange here affect the general morality of the public?…Our schools
are doing much to solve the problem of assimilation…The children of the
immigrant therefore we may have no fear for as regards the future. But the
older people, their parents, is where the problem comes.*

Exactly one week before Edgar Rice and Zachariah Walker's fateful
confrontation near the bridge crossing the Brandywine, at the start of
the Harvest Home Festival, the newspaper editorialized: "Residents of
Coatesville can well appreciate the social changes that are taking place in
America and by reason of the influx of foreign-born people…At first glance
the prospect does not look very encouraging, especially in Coatesville…The
foreigner here is 'cussed' more, probably than any other class. The reason
for this is that we see only the bad side of him, the police court side, the
whiskey drinking and carousing side."

Perhaps the clearest expression of resentment toward the newcomers
came in an anonymous letter to the editor of the *Record*, carried on the front
page of the paper one week after the lynching. The writer had challenged
the editors to print it, convinced that they would not have the courage to do
so. (This may have been a ploy by the editors and interested parties within
the community to disguise a further rationalization of events under the
mantle of the "Defender.") The letter began:

*The fact of the matter is, that although we have always had a certain
amount of lawlessness it has been very small considering the number of
colored and foreigners that are employed in the iron mills. Insult has been
reaped upon injury by those two races and the citizens of this town have
been compelled to take it for several years. Both races have practically
gone over the town roughshod until the people, good American citizens,
were goaded into doing something desperate once the signal was given. It*

can truthfully be said that many persons have been openly insulted by both classes time and again until it developed into a maddened crowd last Sunday evening.

By the summer of 1911, Coatesville was a community divided. Clear-cut political factions within the borough council reflected changing economic and social conditions. A rebellious workingman's group that believed that downtown merchants had too much control over borough politics surfaced in 1910–11 as the most likely challenge to the reigning political power in the town. Edgar Rice was expected to champion their cause in the autumn primary, a brilliant stroke of political opportunism on his part. In the middle stood Charles E. Umsted, whose greatest political virtue was his ability to avoid being identified with any one faction and thereby jeopardize his long-standing tenure as borough police chief.

African American laborers repairing Main Street, Coatesville, 1911. *Courtesy of the Frank Pennegar Collection and the Chester County Historical Society.*

Deeply ingrained class and caste divisions also existed within the larger community, a direct result of Coatesville's status as an industrial town. Substantial differentiation in income and standard of living throughout the borough translated into conditions of social status, relegating a few privileged families to a position of importance. The Worth brothers and the members of the Huston family were the acknowledged leaders of local society, a position guaranteed them by their control of their respective family corporations, Worth Brothers and Lukens Steel. These families were also the town's chief philanthropists, using their wealth and position to sponsor numerous civic and charitable institutions. Theirs was a world of position and power, well removed from the lives of those who toiled in the mills for ten to fifteen dollars a week. Coatesville had its proverbial mansions on the hill and its working-class districts, and the two were separated by more than money, but what all residents had in common was a mutual dependence on the mills for the maintenance of their welfare.

Dr. Charles Huston and his sons with office staff at Lukens Steel. *Courtesy of the Lukens Archives and the Chester County Historical Society.*

"An American Tragedy"

The presence in the borough of large numbers of European immigrants and southern blacks created the greatest divisions. Ethnic and racial antagonism ran high in Coatesville and played directly into the events of August 12–13, 1911. Charles Umsted provided the most succinct summary of the situation when he told the grand jury in September: "In this town, with that population—there is not, in my judgment, there is not a town in the Universe that has the floating population that Coatesville has and that element of people. There are about forty some hundred foreigners there and about two thousand colored people, and the floating element is going…You know, 'Familiarity breeds contempt,' they say." Much the same sentiment was expressed regularly by the local press during the several years preceding the lynching, suggesting the popular belief that Coatesville was a town whose established way of life, whose traditional patterns of everyday interactions, was under assault.

Coatesville retained many of the features of a small town even as it experienced the accelerated changes of the early twentieth century. Popular perceptions of an established order did not evolve to meet the new industrial reality, and consequently the presence of an ever-increasing number of foreigners and southern blacks posed innumerable problems, not the least of which was a challenge to the very meaning of *community*. It would be an understatement to say that the public institutions—the borough council and the police department among them—were incapable of dealing with the problems that attended the transformation of Coatesville. Poorly graded streets, uncollected garbage, an inadequate water supply that bred typhoid fever and parasites and the constant irritant of wild dogs roaming the streets unmolested were but a few of the problems that plagued the town. And, of course, there was the wayward conduct of the newcomers. In fact, by the end of the first decade of the twentieth century, virtually every social problem in Coatesville, from displays of public drunkenness to an increase in violent crime, was blamed on the newly arrived workers. Few people would have been satisfied with an explanation that traced breakdowns in public order to the great social and economic reorganization that was occurring, regardless of the peoples involved. Still fewer residents could have appreciated the extent to which the steel mills manipulated the situation to facilitate their own corporate needs. However, just about everybody agreed that the town was losing control of the situation.

When Zachariah Walker met Edgar Rice on a darkened road on the outskirts of Coatesville, something of a siege mentality already was present in the community. It was as if psychology (individual and collective) was waiting for circumstance, and that occasion came when a recently arrived southern black man killed a popular white policeman in what may have been an act of self-defense. That Rice was seen as a symbol of authority, a representative of the established civil and corporate order in Coatesville, is significant and certainly contributed to how townspeople judged the incident. It is also meaningful that Rice was killed on a Saturday evening and that Walker was likely drunk at the time and was carrying a concealed weapon. The incident was atypical of all the skirmishes that had occurred between the police and the residents of Rock Run, Bernardtown and the Spruces, and in the hearts and minds of many longtime residents it was more than just another moment of confrontation in what Kai Erikson has called the "ongoing social process." As defined by the inhabitants of Coatesville, Walker was an outsider, a "deviant" in the classic sense. (One Pennsylvania newspaper referred to him as a "negro desperado," though it admitted that little was actually known about him.) Not only had he apparently broken the law in killing Rice, but he had deviated from the norm of acceptable conduct for blacks in Coatesville. Walker had stepped out of his "place" in this society; his was an offense against the public order. The slaying of Edgar Rice signaled that a new boundary in the web of community relations had been crossed, and the townspeople were determined to do something about it.

The lynching of Zachariah Walker had a profound effect on the community, bringing to the surface conflicting loyalties that were tied to the very nature of the social circumstances that surrounded the crime. Certain boundaries were ingrained in the everyday life of the borough, and in the weeks and months that followed the lynching, these boundaries were at least partially redrawn as residents attempted to come to terms with what had happened. It makes no sense, however, to interpret Walker's death from a *class* perspective. If anything, the lynching transcended class lines. Judging from the occupational backgrounds of Walker and those identified as witnesses (and perhaps participants), there is no evidence to suggest that the more well-to-do or better-positioned residents had a different attitude about the episode than the average puddler in the mill. Those who did have qualms of conscience or who were embarrassed for the community resigned themselves to the same silence in public that afflicted most of Coatesville's citizens. No one came to Walker's defense, either during or after his ordeal.

One of the more striking consequences of the lynching was the degree of solidarity it forged among native whites and the immigrants. This is not to suggest that longtime residents suddenly embraced the newly arrived Europeans. But newspaper accounts and other sources indicate that, in the weeks following Walker's death, the harshness of rhetoric toward the white foreigners began to soften. The *Record* and other Chester County newspapers still reported instances of wayward behavior by the "foreign element" in Rock Run and Bernardtown, but the articles were less frequent in number. At the same time, the folk customs and traditions of these people were presented in a more sympathetic light, no longer the crude practices of primitive outsiders. In December 1911, the *Record* commented favorably on the holiday festivities being observed in Rock Run and the Spruces, characterizing the immigrants as possessing something of a childlike innocence that only required a degree of detached amusement to appreciate. This was a new spirit of tolerance by a local press that had previously vilified the transplanted European population for its disruptive conduct. In time, these same Europeans and their descendants would be praised for their diligence and their acceptance of the work ethic—a far cry from the sentiments that greeted their arrival in the borough.

There were immigrants in the crowd the night Walker was burned to death. But aside from a rumor that circulated the following day (August 14), no immigrant was ever suspected of being involved in the plot to seize Walker; and after the lynching, no statement of protest, no comment of any kind, came from the immigrant communities (though some native white residents did fear that the foreigners might divulge information during the investigation). Despite their common plight with the southern blacks in Coatesville, the immigrants—including those who may have been troubled by the lynching—saw nothing to gain in coming to Walker's aid. The lynching forged a hitherto unknown unity among the disparate elements of this industrial community's white population. Race, not class or ethnicity, determined how white inhabitants responded to the turmoil. Native whites, for whom race was the single unifying force in the midst of social crisis, at least temporarily defusing class and ethnic hostility, closed ranks with immigrant whites, who in turn took on a new respectability. In the aftermath of the lynching, the *Record* did not miss the opportunity to report on any confrontation with racial overtones, and it was replete with articles on the misconduct and violence of recent black migrants.

Local black reaction to the lynching was shaped by the fact that Walker had recently arrived from rural Virginia. By the summer of 1911, there was a division within the African American community in Coatesville, a distinction based upon the length of time individuals and their families had resided in the town. Instead of embracing the ever-increasing number of southern blacks who found their way to Coatesville, established black citizens kept the newcomers at arm's length, for they had grown increasingly wary of the migrants' potential to undermine whatever social and economic advantage they had achieved. On the eve of the lynching, native whites had come to see southern blacks as strangers in a strange land, and they, too, drew a careful distinction between the newcomers and longtime black residents. Following the lynching, the *Coatesville Times* made this same distinction between "the black man, who behaves himself and is a peaceable law-abiding citizen," and "the lawless black brutes from the South." Referring specifically to Walker as "the brute," the newspaper went on to acknowledge that "everything begets its own kind, and thus it follows that crime begets crime." Although local blacks would not have accepted the newspaper's characterization of the migrants, the wayward conduct of the inhabitants of Rock Run and the Spruces served to qualify whatever bond they may have had to their southern brothers and sisters.

Except for a mild resolution authored by a group of black ministers and shopkeepers, which condemned equally the murder of Edgar Rice and the lynching of Zachariah Walker, the local black community did not respond publicly to the atrocity of August 13. To attribute this reticence to a fear of reprisals is to overlook the existing network of social relationships within Coatesville. In this instance, race identity instilled no special loyalty. Contrary to the *Record*'s account, it was not Prophet Jones's prediction of an impending disaster that explained black quiescence. Where the lynching had galvanized solidarity based on race identification within the white population, it had the opposite effect for blacks, exposing instead a deep-seated division among the black populations and revealing conflicting loyalties. According to a popular expression of the day, Walker may have been *skinfolk*, but he was not *kinfolk*.

Had Walker been familiar to the townspeople, he might not have met the same fate; surely, if he had been a local man, his conduct on the evening of August 12 would not have fit into the social context that lent such immediate importance to the slaying of Edgar Rice. When asked what might have happened to Walker had he been born and raised in Coatesville, a prominent white attorney who grew up in the borough and remembered the lynching was certain that he would not have been lynched and that his plea of self-defense would have carried greater weight with the authorities. Based upon the existing evidence, this seems to be a reasonable conclusion and in fact is the reason why the lynching cannot be separated from the existing social circumstances. Walker *was* an outsider; he was also black and a newcomer. As such, he lived on the margin of local society and its accepted customs. His identification as the assailant immediately triggered a world of meaning and association with which blacks and whites were all too familiar.

When Zachariah Walker killed Edgar Rice, in the eyes of townsfolk he did more than commit a crime. Walker violated the established racial etiquette, and he compounded his mistake when he later confessed that he had killed Rice in self-defense. By doing so, he assumed a measure of equality for himself that the citizens of Coatesville were not willing to accept. When placed on a continuum of ongoing confrontations between established residents and newcomers, especially instances of black-white conflict, the meaning of the Walker lynching is brought clearly into focus. This horrible episode of vigilantism served to maintain certain community values in a time of fundamental social reorganization, while at the same time redefining the meaning of inequality. Southern black migrants might live in or near Coatesville, but they were not a part of Coatesville.

The most difficult thing to explain about a lynching is the act itself and how seemingly ordinary people can behold such a spectacle with ease. To say that in unusual circumstances ordinary people will act in an extraordinary manner provides little insight into the psychology of lynching. Many of the onlookers near Newlin's farm that Sunday evening were there out of curiosity, and perhaps it is unreasonable to expect individuals to stand against so large a mob. After all, the history is replete with instances of mass violence, and few are the voices that objected at the moment. For each person who watched Walker being burned alive, there came a moment when he or she had to choose between staying and walking away, between watching and covering his or her eyes. There were few people who turned away in horror or revulsion; quite the contrary, all accounts of the episode remarked on the politeness of the crowd that night. But at some point the bystanders needed to reconcile the events before them. And it was then that the members of the crowd came to see Walker as an object, as something other than a human being, for their own psychological and emotional well-being. There was a considerable degree of individual self-deception at work in the Walker lynching, and it was the community's collective self-deception that contributed to the success of the "conspiracy of silence" as outside agencies began their investigation.

In the early part of the twentieth century, Coatesville, like other northern steel towns, was permeated by a culture of violence that fostered a peculiar notion of chivalry. This, in turn, made people particularly sensitive to criticism and assault, especially when they were fueled by alcohol. Work in the steel mills was fraught with danger, debilitating injuries were a constant concern and fatal accidents were an ever-present reality. Leisure also carried the potential for violence, especially when it centered on the saloon. Two of the greatest concerns in Coatesville in 1911 were the amount of off-hour drinking in taverns and unlicensed gin joints and the number of persons

Pennsylvania Historical Marker dedicated December 2006. The final marker text recognizes the death of Edgar Rice and the lynching of Zachariah Walker. Nearly two hundred people attended the dedication. *Courtesy of the author.*

who carried concealed firearms. Saturday nights were particularly raucous, and by the summer of 1911, Coatesville's reputation as a tough town had spread beyond Chester County. When a Russian immigrant was detained in Philadelphia one year later, he explained to immigration officials that he was carrying a concealed revolver because he had been hired to work in Coatesville and "was told to bring it" for self-protection.

The average steel town in the early 1900s was clearly a "man's place," as one scholar has observed, and expressions of physical prowess and violent behavior by the young men in town were symbolic of their coming of age. Manhood could not be assumed; it had to be demonstrated, earned and defended when challenged. A man's status in society was confirmed in the company of other men, and the reputation for toughness and a willingness to stand up to a challenge were prized attributes. No man wanted to be branded a coward, perhaps the worst insult he could suffer at the hands of other men. Significantly, nearly half of the defendants in the lynching trials were under the age of twenty-one, and numerous observers had stated that the teenage boys at the front of the mob were the most agitated and had to be cautioned by older men in the crowd to temper their bravado lest they attract the attention of the police. For the young men who participated in the burning of Zachariah Walker and then bragged openly of their accomplishment, the events of August 13 served as a rite of passage, a ritual in which they asserted their manhood by the public display of vengeful force.

That the lynching in Coatesville resulted from the residents' perceived threat to their way of life cannot be denied. Those who participated in the crime claimed they were acting with a higher purpose, one the community at large would sanction. Their behavior was not wild or irrational; rather, it seemed to them to be both reasonable and justified. The mentality of vigilantism—whereby the more extreme the threat to society, the more repressive the punishment inflicted by those who claim to be acting for the public good—was clearly present that night in Coatesville. And, in a sense, so too was the sense of community *honor*.

"Honor," Elliott Gorn has written, "is an intensely social concept, resting on reputation, community standing, and the esteem of kin and compatriots. To possess honor requires acknowledgement from others; it cannot exist in solitary conscience." According to Julian Pitt-Rivers, honor is a masculine trait that governs public relationships and social etiquette "where the law [is] either not competent or not welcome." The code of honor puts a premium on the individual's reputation in the eyes of others, and to have one's character impugned in public is an occasion of shame that demands a response; indeed, the one who suffered the affront has the right to demand satisfaction. Honor is also a community value that dictates absolute loyalty to family and kin that solidifies the members of opposing groups. A "willingness to stand up to opposition is essential to the acquisition, as to the defense, of honor," Pitt-Rivers has noted, *regardless of the mode of action that is adopted.*

Without disputing historians' claims for the importance of honor in the nineteenth-century American South, it is worth noting that a potentially lethal combination of violence, honor and an exaggerated notion of manhood was very much in play in the Walker lynching. For all of its accelerated growth in the early 1900s, Coatesville remained in many respects a small town, a "family place" that lacked the anonymity of more cosmopolitan cities. This intimacy among established residents provided a source of cohesion during the decade of adjustment that preceded the lynching, despite obvious class and status differences. And it made honor, and its connection to masculinity and cowardice, a potent force in male social relationships—so much so, in fact, that in certain situations an affront to one man could be judged as an affront to all.

Those who killed Zachariah Walker in retribution for the death of Edgar Rice claimed that they were securing satisfaction for the widow and her children, and for the community at large. What the leaders of the mob saw as *justice* for Walker's affront to the public order was in fact a form of vigilantism that reaffirmed their own status as well as community boundaries. But this was also an instance of "rough justice," to borrow Michael Pfeifer's apt expression, that did not respect the formal legal process.

The prevailing psychology was such that moderation and recourse to the courts would not suffice. A man was expected to do the "honorable thing," not only by the dead man's family but by his fellow men, and he was expected to do it promptly. To wait for the law to deal with Rice's murderer would have been a sign of weakness, something that was not acceptable in this situation. So, too, would it have been unthinkable to allow the widow to participate in the deed, despite her willingness to strike the match.

These sentiments were not manufactured on the spur of the moment but were deeply embedded in the culture of Coatesville. And what better and more complete a statement about Walker's deviance, his honor-less status, than to destroy his very person by burning him alive? What is also striking was the absolute normality of the episode for those who participated in the lynching—indeed, the apparent absence of any frenzy or trauma in the crowd as Walker suffered his painful ordeal.

Perhaps the ultimate irony of this episode is that the honor of Coatesville was resurrected in Walker's charred and broken bones. "People scratched in ashes with bare hands for relics of lynching of murderer," a newspaper caption read, and the *Record* reporter at the scene likened the scavengers to "a pack of hungry wolves after a morsel of food." "Those having the relics exhibited them in glee," he noted. "The small boy was foremost in this demonstration and before he got away from the scene was offering for sale and finding purchasers for the gruesome relics." While collecting and selling such souvenirs on street corners is disquieting, indeed barbaric, it was commonplace after burnings and lynchings in earlier times, and most residents of Coatesville apparently found nothing perverse in the practice. Clearly, the human capacity for self-deception, the ability to see things as other than they are, was a potent force in rationalizing the lynching. Although the inhabitants of the borough remained extremely sensitive to any criticism in the weeks following the incident, the assaults from outside Coatesville seemed to reinforce the conviction from within that what had happened was tragic but understandable, a reasonable response given the existing conditions.

Miss Norma Eaby, a longtime resident of Coatesville, was one of the many people who heard the commotion of the lynch mob that fateful Sunday evening. Leaving her porch step on West Chestnut Street to follow the crowd as it proceeded from the hospital, she heard a man up in front say to Walker, "You killed Edgar Rice, you ----- -----! You were in Coatesville last night! You were in the hospital tonight! You will be in the furnace soon! And you will be in hell tomorrow!" On hearing this remark, Walker was confronted with his destiny.

The danger of such a view was that the mob became a collective repository of moral authority and that responsibility for its actions did not fall on individual members. In putting Walker to death, the *community* reenacted what had become a commonplace ritual elsewhere in the country, namely, exorcising the demon and redeeming virtue. This was an episode in which community won out over conscience, and for that reason a group of teenage boys could boast to one another with a confidence that belied their age, "We made a good job of it!" and then set off for the soda shop to quench their thirst. Tomorrow was indeed another day, and the mills would open on time.

AFTERWORD

The lynching death of Zachariah Walker was an extraordinary event rooted in the ordinary, everyday life of citizens in one Pennsylvania steel town. But it is also a historical moment that permits close inspection of the broader patterns of social and economic change in early twentieth-century America, to say nothing of the fault line of race and rights in modern American history. Though its geographic location in southeastern Pennsylvania contradicts the presumption that lynching was a uniquely southern phenomenon tied to a particular regional culture of violence, in many respects the Coatesville incident was representative of the larger commonplace reality of spectacle lynchings. It is also noteworthy that the memory of this episode of mob violence continues to reverberate within the community one hundred years later.

Within months of the final acquittals, Governor John K. Tener called on the state legislature to revoke the Borough of Coatesville's municipal charter. "People of this Borough," he declared in his 1913 annual address, "by fomenting murder and consorting with murderers have not only violated the laws and obstructed the administration of justice, but in my judgment have forfeited the high privilege of further acting as a governmental agency of the State." By their actions, the inhabitants of Coatesville—officials and citizens—had assured that the commonwealth would be "disgraced and her fair name dishonored." Strong words from a relatively inexperienced executive, and they were not well received by constituents in Chester County.

Despite a rising tide of outrage, legislators balked at the governor's notion of revoking the privilege of self-government.

As the General Assembly debated Tener's recommendation, a curious defense of local residents appeared in the February 1913 issue of *The Cresset Magazine*, a small periodical published in Chester County. Written by Wayne Morris and titled "Coatesville, from a Coatesville Point of View," the essay sought to move "beyond the superficial understanding of the Scribes and Pharisees." Morris saw the lynching as the result of agitation by the "lower elements of humanity" who were exasperated by existing conditions. "Humanity is not infallible," he argued. "There are potential lynchers in every community in the United States, to say nothing of the rest of the world." And what of the mob's motivation? "It was not lawlessness," he observed. "It was the exact opposite; it was justice! Their inner being cried out in the heat of inflamed passion, 'Justice!' That is all the lynching of Zack [*sic*] Walker was, the cry of the lower element of humanity for justice... They were the people, and the law was made by the people and is always subservient to their will." What Morris described as a jury of "good men and true" would not permit their "manhood" to pass the sentence of death on the accused, half of whom were boys.

Where Governor Tener found the incident a betrayal of democracy and human decency, Morris's lengthy apologia claimed the opposite. Democracy and a particular understanding of justice itself had triumphed in the "will of the people" throughout the ordeal. "Coatesville rejoiced," Morris asserted of the celebratory mood that followed the last trials, "because mere victims of chance did not have to suffer in place of the real lynchers." It was one thing to rationalize the conduct of the perpetrators and quite another to suggest that it was all a case of mistaken identity. In the juxtaposition of the governor's address and the journalist's article, the unorthodox debate about race and rights, democracy and vigilante justice that shaped American attitudes toward lynching came into sharp relief.

More than any other civil rights organization in the country, the NAACP followed events in the borough and kept its expanding membership informed of the outcome of the trials. In June 1912, *The Crisis* printed an editorial titled "Triumph" in which W.E.B. Du Bois reminded readers that the previous September he had predicted a failure of justice in Pennsylvania. Now, Du Bois wrote with added bitterness, "the last lyncher is acquitted and the best traditions of Anglo-Saxon civilization are safe...Let the eagle

W.E.B. Du Bois. *Courtesy of the Library of Congress.*

scream!" Despite his expressed frustration, the association continued to be active behind the scenes in an attempt to bring the lynchers to justice.

In a series of meetings between September 1912 and February 1913, NAACP representatives met with Governor Tener and Deputy Attorney General Jesse Cunningham in the hopes of persuading them to reopen the cases. Oswald Garrison Villard, legal counsel William Wherry and several others presented them with new evidence, including the names of alleged unindicted participants, that their investigators had uncovered. In a further effort to change the commonwealth's position, Attorney General John Bell was invited to New York in late January to discuss the matter with the NAACP's board of directors, but he declined the offer. All of this occurred prior to Tener's address to the legislature. Despite an apparent interest in supporting the NAACP's request, Governor Tener chose not to renew the prosecutions.

Having failed in this attempt, the NAACP altered its strategy and became the chief advocate for an antilynching law in Pennsylvania. Within weeks of Tener's decision not to reopen the lynching cases, NAACP attorneys drafted legislation that Representative Samuel Scott, a liberal Republican from Philadelphia's Fifteenth District and a direct descendant of Benjamin Franklin, introduced to the general assembly on March 17, 1913. (In this same session, a bill prohibiting interracial marriage was introduced but never became law.) The antilynching bill, which was in response to the Coatesville incident, was modeled on legislation in Illinois and Ohio and listed specific statutory sanctions for those who engaged in mob violence. Wherry and his successor, Chapin Brinsmade, worked with Scott for over one year to resolve constitutional issues raised by the legislation, particularly those regarding the liability of public officials who turned their backs on mob violence. In a foreshadowing of the problems faced by the federal antilynching bill proposed during World War I, the Pennsylvania bill took ten years to clear both legislative houses. Governor Gifford Pinchot signed into law a version of Scott's original proposal on May 19, 1923, but by that time many people had forgotten the episode that demonstrated the necessity of such a measure.

The brutal murder of Zachariah Walker was one of the first cases the NAACP became directly involved in as part of its effort to end lynching in the United States. That it was a northern lynching made the episode especially important to the association, for in highlighting Walker's fate in Coatesville, the civil rights organization was allowed to emphasize the *national* character of the "race question" without appearing to be simply anti-southern in its position. Ironically, the Walker lynching was used by southern editorialists to demand that northern commentators examine their own consciences lest they apply a double standard to black-white relations. The NAACP's failure to win mass support in the North for its antilynching campaign and the repeated failure of the U.S. Congress to pass the Dyer Anti-Lynching Bill in the early 1920s were serious defeats for the organization.

The story is told that on a hot summer's day not long after the lynching trials had ended, a group of white boys was playing ball in a field near the East End in Coatesville. A young black child was playing by himself at the opposite end of the same park. When the boys saw the youth, they approached him and threatened to start a fire and burn him alive, just like Walker had been, if he did not leave immediately. The black child fled in terror, leaving behind a group of white boys who laughed with delight at their prank. That same summer, the Worth Brothers Company completed the construction of a large dormitory "to house colored laborers coming from the South." As the local mills returned to full productivity in the summer of 1912, labor agents contracted for hundreds of new southern black migrants to journey north. "The men are the laborers brought here by the iron mills and are quartered in the houses owned by the mills," noted the *Coatesville Record* of the population surge in Rock Run and Bernardtown.

Despite the widespread attention the Walker lynching received, Coatesville's connection with the rural South continued over the next decades. Depressed economic conditions in the Southeast and the lure of regular employment and better wages in Coatesville overrode other concerns for those who chose to cast their lot with the local mills. With America's entry into World War I, the demand for labor in steel mills and other factories increased dramatically across the North. This demand acted as a magnet drawing more and more southern blacks northward as European immigration slackened. Pennsylvania remained "the single most attractive state for northbound blacks" between 1910 and 1920, according to one study, and Coatesville received its share of these newcomers. During the war years, more than two thousand newly arrived southern black migrants lived in company housing or in the dozen or more "labor camps" created on farms in the townships that surrounded Coatesville. Like the earlier generation of migrants to the borough, these men were intentionally kept at a safe distance from the established neighborhoods and main thoroughfares of the community.

While most historians have put special emphasis on the increased outmigration from the South in the years 1915 to 1917, it would be a mistake to separate the experience of these migrants from those who came before them. Too often overlooked is the continuity of the migration experience in the North, from its earliest inception at the turn of the century. What few observers realized at the time, and what is abundantly clear in hindsight, is that the Walker lynching in Coatesville was not some fluke, some isolated occurrence. Even though Wayne Morris overstated the situation when he said that there were "potential lynchers in every community" in the United States, he had a point. A pattern of racial violence in the North has sustained itself in various forms throughout the twentieth century, a century marked by the ebb and flow of blacks and poor whites from the South to the promised land of the urban-industrial North.

In July 1917, in the midst of American mobilization for the war, a violent race riot erupted in East St. Louis, Illinois. Two weeks later, a similar riot broke out in Chester, Pennsylvania, an industrial town not far from Coatesville. The next summer, a much larger urban race riot rocked

Philadelphia, foreshadowing the pattern of interracial violence in major cities across the country during the Red Summer of 1919. In March 1919, as troops returned home from the European campaign, word of racial troubles in Coatesville reached the New York offices of the NAACP. The *New York Post*, published by Oswald Garrison Villard, reported that black workers were being forcibly deported from Coatesville. On behalf of the association, Secretary John Shillady cabled telegrams to William Wilson, secretary of the U.S. Department of Labor, to the governor of Pennsylvania and to the mayor of Coatesville demanding an explanation and an official inquiry. The Labor Department sent an investigator, who arrived in Coatesville at about the same time as Assistant Secretary Walter White of the NAACP. White reported that some thirty-three hundred black workers were presently employed by Lukens and by the Midvale Steel and Ordnance Company, which had taken control of Worth Brothers in 1916 and was itself purchased by Lukens in the 1930s. Many of the newly arrived blacks, and some white laborers as well, were not put to work immediately but were kept in company housing for days without pay. Some apparently committed petty thefts to survive. "No decent colored man had been molested," the pastor of Olivet ME Church assured White, who in turn concluded that the press had blown things out of proportion.

In a separate letter to an associate, White repeated his conviction that the local officials had done nothing improper. "On going to Coatesville," he wrote, "I found that conditions there were not as bad as the newspaper reports had stated, but that the men who had been run out of town, both white and colored, were not the type which worked, but the gambling and loafing element." Indeed, he had received assurances from Mayor S.H. Wing that both white and black "undesirables" were being "rounded up and given fifteen minutes to get out of town." Furthermore, White noted in his report to the NAACP, it was apparent that the public attitude of Coatesville's officials had softened toward recent black migrants. Hardworking, law-abiding blacks were welcome in the city, the mayor had told him, although the "floating element" was still viewed with contempt. Wing insisted, "We need the Negro here in Coatesville, and will do nothing to hurt him." In addition, it was pointed out that three of the nine men on the Coatesville police force were black—one from Virginia and the other two from North Carolina. The mayor told White that the area in which the greatest number of "loafers" congregated was East Fallowfield Township, just outside the city limits. This happened to be the same area where Zachariah Walker and Edgar Rice had their fateful confrontation eight summers earlier.

Twenty-seven years after Walker's death, a second lynching in Coatesville was averted, thanks to a courageous police chief. In June 1938, a young white woman, a teenager from the community, was attacked on South Hill. Word quickly spread that her assailant was black, and a posse spread out to search the surrounding countryside. Within several hours, a young black man was apprehended and brought to the city jail, now located opposite the Lukens mill. A crowd was waiting by the entrance to the police station, and as the posse arrived, words that were familiar to an older generation of residents were heard. Several voices called for the accused to be lynched, but this time the chief of police demonstrated the kind of courage that a former constable had lacked. Ralph Williams stood against the crowd on the lawn and said that justice demanded better of them. Coatesville did not need a repetition of the drama of 1911. On hearing these words, the crowd grew silent, and its members wandered away without protest. When it was safe to do so, Williams and his deputies took the accused to a nearby city for better protection. Several days later, the police arrested a white man who confessed to the crime.

In 1973, a group of black steelworkers filed a class action lawsuit against Lukens Steel in Coatesville. These laborers, themselves migrants from the South or the children of migrants, charged that for decades the steel company had followed a systematic pattern of job discrimination, consciously excluding blacks from certain types of jobs and avenues of advancement. Eleven years later, in December 1984, a U.S. District Court judge found for the plaintiffs. In addition to acknowledging the policy of job discrimination in the Coatesville mills, Judge John P. Fullam commented on the practice of harassment of black workers that the union locals had done nothing to oppose. In July 1985, Lukens offered the more than thirteen hundred black workers affected by the decision a settlement of $3.7 million, one-third of which would be claimed by attorneys for their work. Several of the plaintiffs objected to that division, inasmuch as they saw it as a further injustice, but in the end the settlement was accepted.

In the two decades following the historic settlement, Coatesville's social and economic landscape changed significantly. On the one hand, deindustrialization and the declining economy of steel have wounded the community. The once mighty industrial economy has gone through a fundamental transformation, the mills have been sold several times and the job market has shrunken. On the other hand, the area immediately outside the city proper has developed into a bedroom community of sorts for working professionals who make the daily commute into Philadelphia. This tale of two cities reinforces Coatesville's relevance to a larger American narrative, now cast forward into the twenty-first century.

On a crisp winter's day in December 2006, nearly two hundred residents from across Chester County attended a public meeting that coincided with the dedication of a state historical marker near the lynching site. Not so much a reconciliation but a remembrance service, the community forum was an interracial public witness to the lingering controversy surrounding August 13, 1911. Neither a gesture toward healing nor closure, the marker itself documents those events and their importance in Pennsylvania and American history. Though some objected at the time, organizers agreed to the inclusion of a mention of Edgar Rice's death in the marker text as an appropriate recognition of the depth of the tragedy of that "quiet Sabbath evening" so many summers ago. The marker still stands on donated land on the outskirts of Coatesville.

To the man, those accused in the lynching of Zachariah Walker faded into obscurity, living out their lives in quiet anonymity. The controversy surrounding the lynching brought to an end Charles Umsted's lengthy tenure as constable of Coatesville. Stanley Howe never achieved the prominence he desired. Edgar Rice is buried in the shadow of Hephzibah Baptist Church, on a gentle rolling hill below Coatesville. A new tombstone marks his grave. No one knows what became of Zachariah Walker's remains, though it is certain that neither his family nor anyone else claimed them for a proper burial. They have been lost in the passage of time, and now he, like they, is left to memory and to history.

BIBLIOGRAPHY

PRIMARY SOURCES

Chester County Courthouse Archives, West Chester, PA. *Grand Jury Investigation, Coatesville Lynching.*

Court of Oyer and Terminer and General Jail, October 1911 and May 1912.

Library of Congress, Washington, D.C. Papers of the National Association for the Advancement of Colored People.

National Archives, Washington, D.C. Census materials, 1890–1920.

Pennsylvania State Archives, Harrisburg, PA. Department of State Police *Annual Reports* (1911 and 1912) for Troop C. Municipal Records Collection. Minutes of the Borough Council (Coatesville).

———. Minutes of the Chester County Commission.

Pennsylvania Supreme Court, Record Group 33, January term 1912.

Newspapers

Boston Guardian
Chicago Defender
Coatesville Record
Coatesville Times
Coatesville Weekly Times
Daily Clarion Ledger (Jackson, MS)

Harrisburg Telegraph
Indianapolis Freeman
Johnstown Leader
Johnstown Weekly Democrat
Lancaster Intelligencer
Lebanon Daily News
Memphis Commercial Appeal
New York Age
New York Times
Philadelphia Bulletin
Philadelphia Inquirer
Philadelphia Press
Pittsburgh Courier
Pittsburgh Dispatch
Richmond Times (VA)
The State (Columbia, SC)
Steelton Press
Washington Bee
Washington Post
West Chester Daily Local News

Magazines

The American Magazine
The Cresset Magazine
The Crisis
The Nation
The Outlook
Southern Workman

SELECTED SECONDARY SOURCES

Allen, James, et al. *Without Sanctuary: Lynching Photography in America.* Santa Fe, NM: Twin Palms, 2008.

Brundage, W. Fitzhugh. *Lynching in the New South: Georgia and Virginia, 1880–1930.* Urbana: University of Illinois Press, 1993.

———, ed. *Under Sentence of Death: Lynching in the South.* Chapel Hill: University of North Carolina Press, 1997.

Carrigan, William. *Lynching Reconsidered: New Perspectives in the Study of Mob Violence.* New York: Routledge, 2008.

Collins, Winfield H. *The Truth about Lynching and the Negro in the South.* New York: Neale Publishing Company, 1918.

Cutler, James. *Lynch-Law.* New York: Longmans, Green, and Company, 1905.

Dickerson, Dennis. *Out of the Crucible: Black Steelworkers in Western Pennsylvania, 1875–1980.* Albany: State University of New York Press, 1986.

Downey, Dennis B., and Raymond M. Hyser. "'A Crooked Death': Coatesville, Pennsylvania, and the Lynching of Zachariah Walker." *Pennsylvania History* 54 (April 1987): 85–102.

Dray, Philip. *At the Hands of Persons Unknown: The Lynching of Black America.* New York: Random House, 2002.

Durkheim, Emile. *The Division of Labor in Society.* New York: Free Press, 1984.

Erikson, Kai. *Everything in Its Path: Destruction of Community in the Buffalo Creek Flood.* New York: Simon and Schuster, 1976.

———. *Wayward Puritans: A Study in the Sociology of Deviance.* New York: Wiley, 1966.

Giddings, Paula. *Ida: A Sword Among Lions: Ida B. Wells and the Campaign Against Lynching.* New York: Amistad, 2009.

Goldman, Eric. "Summer Sunday." *American Heritage* 15 (June 1964): 50–53, 83–89.

Gottlieb, Peter. *Making Their Own Way: Southern Blacks' Migration to Pittsburgh, 1916–30.* Urbana: University of Illinois Press, 1987.

Henri, Florette. *Black Migration: Movement North, 1900–1920.* Garden City, NY: Anchor Press, 1975.

Huggins, Nathan, ed. *W.E.B. Du Bois: Writings.* New York: Viking Press, 1986.

Hunt, Doug. *Summary Justice: The Lynching of James Scott and the Trial of George Barkwell in Columbia, Missouri.* Charleston, SC: self-published, 2010.

Johnston, Daniel M., and Rex R. Campbell. *Black Migration in America: A Social Demographic History.* Durham, NC: Duke University Press, 1981.

Madison, James. *A Lynching in the Heartland: Race and Memory in America.* New York: Palgrave, 2001.

Marks, Carole. *Farewell—We're Good and Gone: The Great Black Migration.* Bloomington: Indiana University Press, 1989.

NAACP. *Thirty Years of Lynching, 1889–1918*. New York: National Association for the Advancement of Colored People, National Office, 1919.

Pfeifer, Michael. *The Roots of Rough Justice: Origins of American Lynching*. Urbana: University of Illinois Press, 2011.

———. *Rough Justice: Lynching and American Society*. Urbana: University of Illinois Press, 2004.

Raper, Arthur. *The Tragedy of Lynching*. Chapel Hill: University of North Carolina Press, 1933.

Shay, Frank. *Judge Lynch*. New York: I. Washburn, Inc., 1938.

Waldrep, Christopher. *African Americans Confront Lynching: Strategies of Resistance from the Civil War to the Civil Rights Era*. Lanham, MD: Rowan and Littlefield Publishers, 2009.

———. *The Many Faces of Judge Lynch: Extralegal Violence and Punishment in America*. New York: Palgrave Macmillan, 2002.

Wells-Barnett, Ida B. "A Red Record." In *On Lynchings 2*. 1895. Reprint, New York: Arno Press, 1969.

Wexler, Laura. *Fire in the Canebrake: The Last Mass Lynching in America*. New York: Scribner, 2003.

White, Walter. *A Man Called White*. 1948. Reprint, Bloomington: Indiana University Press, 1970.

———. *Rope and Faggot: A Biography of Judge Lynch*. New York: Alfred A. Knopf, 1929.

Wood, Amy. *Lynching and Spectacle: Witnessing Racial Violence in America, 1890–1940*. Chapel Hill: University of North Carolina Press, 2009.

Zangrando, Robert. *The NAACP Crusade against Lynching, 1909–1950*. Philadelphia: Temple University Press, 1980.

Ziglar, William. "'Community on Trial': The Coatesville Lynching of 1911." *Pennsylvania Magazine of History and Biography* 106 (April 1982): 245–70.

ABOUT THE AUTHORS

D ennis B. Downey is professor of history and director of the university honors college at Millersville University (Pennsylvania). He is the author of five books and two book-length web histories, the most recent of which is entitled "The Peopling of Pennsylvania: The Creation of a Multicultural Society" (2011).

R aymond M. Hyser is professor of history and cluster coordinator of the General Education program at James Madison University (Virginia). He is author of three books. He served as chief reader for the Advanced Placement United States History program.

Visit us at
www.historypress.net